GET OFF

— THE —

Shelf

Choose You First, You Have a Right to Be Happy

VICKI L. DOBBS

Get Off the Shelf

Wisdom Evolution
10102 E. Bullard Ave
Clovis Ca 93619
Vickidobbs.Com

Book Design by Transcendent Publishing

ISBN: 978-1-7373404-1-6

Disclaimer: Although the author and publisher have made every effort to ensure that the information in this book was correct at press time, the author and publisher do not assume and hereby disclaim any liability to any party for any loss, damage, or disruption caused by errors or omissions, whether such errors or omissions result from negligence, accident, or any other cause. This book is not intended as a substitute for the medical advice of a medical professional. The reader is advised to regularly consult with a physician in matters relating to his/her health and particularly with respect to any symptoms that may require medical attention. The Deepening Practices found in each chapter are meant for personal use and not as a medical or psychological therapy.

Printed in the United States of America.

This book is dedicated to you, The Reader, for having the curiosity, courage, and strength to look deep within the folds of your own heart and soul.

CONTENTS

*"When life shows itself to be tumultuous,
it's because you are being prepared
for something greater."*

–Usher

FOREWORD

by Lynn V. Andrews

*T*he sound of the drums was calling everyone to the next session of our weekend together. As I walked through the multi-colored layers of gossamer material hanging from the rafters, I was engaged by the drummers lining the walkway. Dancing through the last of the hanging fabric, I saw a woman sitting at a Grandmother Drum, blissed out on the beat, lost in the tempo and tenor of her drum. Our eyes met and I recognized that familiar hesitancy that asked, "Am I doing this right; is it OK for me to be here?" I would get to know Vicki Dobbs over the next few years as she discovered who she was and who she was becoming through the depth of the work she was challenged to complete in my four-year mystery school, The Way of the Wolf.

As a fourth-year apprentice, she faced an unfathomable grief in the loss of her son. I watched her navigate the depths of that darkness, move through completion of her work with me and rise into a new light as she became a mentor in both my schools, a workshop facilitator, teacher, and speaker. I am honored now to call her my friend.

As a New York Times and International best-selling author of more than twenty books, I was at the forefront of the movement to bring awareness to the imbalance between the feminine and masculine energies in our lives. I wrote, taught and lectured, through my stories, how to embody the feminine 'being' nature of woman while maintaining the masculine 'doing' aspect of working in our world today.

Through my books, the mystery school, writing school and my events, I have introduced tens of thousands of readers and students to the process of personal empowerment and self-growth. Vicki has incorporated what she learned with me and other teachers and has written her journey into a model for the everyday busy woman.

In this book, Vicki shares her personal stories from childhood insecurities to getting lost in a world of doing, never being or dreaming herself. In reading her story, you might recognize when you are lost or caught in the fast lane of a life lived unconsciously and discover through her thought provoking and experiential exercises, ways she has developed for "getting off the shelf."

As a Graduate, Mentor, and Administrator of my schools, a Harner trained Shamanic Counselor and Artist of the Spirit Life Coach, Vicki brings that depth of education and experience to each of her clients, classes, and workshops.

Perhaps you have found yourself stuck in your everyday life, set aside by your responsibilities, and feeling invisible to the world around you. Vicki's story will likely touch a familiar place in you as you discover that you are not alone in your struggles. Her use of shamanicly crafted ceremony, sacred art, or the creation of medicine tools in each of her exercises, offers you practical opportunities for finding balance in your life as you discover and master your own ways to get off the shelf.

INTRODUCTION

The future stands open-armed in invitation,
Each step a lifetime's journey
In, out, into myself.
Who I am and who I might become?
Courage doesn't mean anything without purpose and direction.
My life extends far beyond the limitations of me but,
If I were to remain invisible, my truth would stay hidden!
Love endures eternity and repeats itself endlessly
through eons of lessons.
Will they ever believe one can make a difference?
That a single drop in a sea of unconsciousness
will awaken them all?

I was called to write *Get Off the Shelf* during a very visceral dream. I was walking down a long hallway lined with bookshelves when my attention was drawn to movement over my left shoulder. I looked up and saw on the top shelf my agitated self, looking down at me. "What the hell am I doing up here?" she asked. That's when I knew it was time, once again, for me to get off the shelf.

This book is about how we, especially women, set ourselves aside in service to everyone and everything else in our lives except ourselves. In it you will see what an intentionally crafted life looks like; learn ways to recognize when you are lost in a life lived for others; discover tools, techniques, and ceremonies for kickstarting or rebooting your sacred dream; and determine how to get off the shelf once and for all.

I started writing my first book in the seventh grade, a girl's version of the Disney series Spin and Marty. In my little book, the girls, not just the boys, got to go to a western ranch camp. My stories lived in my head but never made it to paper, until now... until a voice yelled at me from the top of a bookshelf. I have written for workshops and seminars. I write prayers, meditations, and guided visualizations. *Get Off the Shelf* is not the story I thought I would write. It is the book I *have* to write.

At first, I thought it was ego-driven, as in "see me?" Now I know it is heart-driven. My heart hurts, and I know that if I want to be happy again, I must remember how. When life is joyless, it is fruitless, and I know in that still place inside that if I do not write now, I will shrivel up and die. And, just maybe, the writing of these stories will heal not only my pain, but the reader's as well.

Let me share a bit about me and how I have come to be in this space. I have been an entrepreneur since the age of eight, when I sold greeting cards door-to-door to earn money for a pup tent to camp out in the backyard. I sold butter toffee peanuts to earn my way to summer camp. In the *Urban Cowboy* era, I worked my way through college by doing custom leatherwork for various western stores.

It was my love of horses that led me to the man I married nearly fifty years ago. Blessed to be a stay-at-home mom, I enjoyed many opportunities to put my teaching education to work in our children's classrooms and on their fields of play as a coach and team mother. I taught children's craft classes in community education programs, and now I teach workshops with a spiritually empowering message that includes art projects for students to anchor these teachings in their physical life.

My mother taught me the value of volunteer work. As a teenager I served as a candy striper at the local hospital and as a crafts teacher at the neighborhood playground. As an adult, I became a part of our community as an advocate and diplomat sitting on the boards for the Foundation for Clovis Schools, the Police Activities League, and the Clovis District Chamber of Commerce.

Success came as a Realtor®, when I got a peek at how I could achieve as me, and not as who I perceived I was supposed to be. I jumped outside the box and did real estate my way, farming people by being with them in the community instead of farming neighborhoods for houses to sell. I was named Clovis Business Professional Woman of the Year in 1999.

Still, I remember being vaguely aware of feeling on the edge of "me"; I didn't know who that really was. Trapped in a world of doing everything for everybody else, I had no idea I could envision a life for me, one that would fuel my joy, set my heart on fire and free my soul's desires. I was in middle age, yet the old voices were still in control, taunting me daily with *"Were those the right words? Is that the right blouse to wear? Oh my God, are you doing that right? What will people think?"* The box I had built around "me" kept out all other possibilities. I was still looking for permission to be happy.

Finally, I quit – stepped off the proverbial hamster's wheel I had been running on and climbed up on a shelf. From there I looked out at the world – agitated, frustrated, sad and afraid, questioning everything I knew as me. Had I lost sight of my dream? And then it hit me right smack in the face: What dream? No one ever told me I could have a dream!

I did pick up the pen again, this time to write a short story. A dear friend and prolific author read it and proclaimed, "You're not a writer, Vicki, you are a storyteller!" I completely missed the gift in those words. *"I'm not a writer,"* I thought, and that was the end of that. I stuck to the workshops I was teaching and to the clients I mentored and coached. I kept selling houses and retreated to my comfy chair. With the loss of our son in 2005, I lost all sense of my boundaries once again, and let that proverbial box define my life. I accepted speaking opportunities and wrote for those moments, those classes, those events. I wrote for them, not for me, not for you, until I heard my own voice scream, "Get me down from here!"

I learned young that doing kept the emotions at bay. Even as I write this, I want to go to sleep. I did that a lot – stayed up late and slept half the day away on weekends. Sleep was a way to escape, to stay up there on that familiar shelf; holding back any part of myself kept me glued there.

The human spirit inside each of us has an enormous capacity to survive every unexpected twist and turn life has to offer. As the darkness of anger, grief and frustration passed through my decision to change and begin again, I understood it had to be a conscious, intentional choice made from the heart and not the head. I think it is written in a song or a movie somewhere that life is not about how to survive the storm, it is about how to dance in the rain. I am not only going to dance, but I am also going to splash around in every puddle, throw my head back and taste the raindrops on my tongue.

"The dream of dreamers dreaming is

In the knowing that they can have A Dream! "

Now, as I walk through my seventh decade, I write for the women living – and the young girls growing up – in this fast-changing world; those who are suddenly thrown into vats of steaming anger and stomach-churning fear or regret or steamrolled by power that keeps telling them to get strong, be strong, but refuses to allow them to be. I write for women like myself, who are living a life bound to WOPT (What Other People Think?) with no vision for themselves of what they want to do or be in this world. They are moving through their days, reacting to each relationship, circumstance, or situation instead of dreaming their own into being. I am writing for the women who never got the message that they could be whatever they wanted to be, to do whatever they wanted to do – outside of boxes and without labels.

Chapter One

LIVING ON THE EDGE
OF AWARENESS

Sunrise was a sudden flare upon the horizon,
As the day drags itself across asphalt ribbons
'Til diamond dust glitters in a blue-black sky looking for
a pale sickle moon.
I cannot live in yesterday. I wish me not to go unarmed
into this world.
Today is not to dream about, it is the Dream, today!

I have been circling "nothing" for the past couple of years while my body spirals out of control: three knee surgeries, weight gain; fighting sleep, fighting respiratory illness, and unrelenting body aches and pains. Selling our family home of forty-plus years implies movement, yes, but I am moving through the days with no drive, no motivation, and no passion. It's all busywork to move time; multitasking to fill space while accomplishing only the bare minimum needed to "keep up" with obligations.

2017 was to be my breakout year. I was filled with drive and ambition, working on my physical body and my own sacred space. Life happened, we were moving, there were boxes everywhere and opinions enough to fill a book but… where had Vicki gone?

I have vacillated, back and forth with this vision, a quest, an opportunity. What do I want to discover, to unfold, to dissect and eliminate, to rebirth, to "see"? The first thing that pops into my mind is this: I want to see "ME." I didn't see this coming. And it's not the "me" of this plane, but the one that has gotten lost again. My power had slipped away and, after Ryan passed, so had my sense of self and boundaries. After that senseless accident in 2005 took him, death stalked our family. Just three months later my god-mother – my mother's best friend of sixty-three years – passed from complications after surgery. My uncle was diagnosed with lung cancer just ninety days after that and passed in October of that same year, 2006. Weeks after my uncle's diagnosis, a dear friend departed in a single car accident, and my oldest brother-in-law left this earth the day after my uncle. My mom announced the following spring that she was "ready to go" and indeed was gone by the end of 2007. In less than three years I had not only lost half the branches from my "tree," but, with the passing of my remaining parent, my very roots. I was teetering to find balance. I had lost my grip on "me." Clearly, getting off the shelf this time was going to take a bigger solution than a good night's sleep. I needed to find a place to just be for a while – listen for a message, for the next move, from a place of serenity and silence.

When I first ventured onto this spiritual path, I had no clue of the power that lay in silence. It had been missing in a life consumed with family, kids, television shows, work, and community. I even turned the soft music on at night to go to sleep. I needed a fan in a room when I traveled. Noise was a constant companion. I don't think I had ever spent any time with myself in silence.

One Friday, I took myself to an all-day real estate tax seminar in Scottsdale, Arizona. I was just a couple of hours from Sedona, so I made a reservation for the weekend at a small hotel – just me, myself, and I. No one else, no agenda.

Early Saturday morning I went for a hike out to some of the native ruins in the area. Sedona's Pink Jeep Tours hadn't yet started that day; only the rangers were present. They left me to stroll and connect with the wisdom and beauty that I found in the silence of this ancient place.

I moved on as the jeeps arrived at the ruins. I headed to Boynton Canyon. Mind you, I was not in the greatest of physical shape, so I had chosen an "easy" hike, to the ruins as it was described in the *Hike Sedona* book I'd found at Safeway. Having handled "easy" I opted for the "moderate" canyon hike – just an hour and a half. The book was a bit outdated, as the Enchanted Resort had since been built in the mouth of the Boynton Canyon and hikers had to go around. Several times I wanted to give up as I was feeling more and more alone on the trail. Two hours in, the shadows grew longer, and my inexperience played scary in my mind. Yet, each time I was about to turn around someone would show up on the trail and encourage me with, "It's just around the corner up there."

A teenage girl came jogging up, having left her mother trailing behind. When she saw me resting against a rock, she asked, "Wanna walk on together? How much farther?"

"I don't have any idea," I replied, "but a couple just went by and said it was just around the next bend or two. I'd love the company." I was happy to have a companion since other hikers were few and far between and I didn't *really* know how much farther it was. Together we agreed we'd go just another ten minutes, since the temperature was beginning to drop and neither of us had jackets.

We made it to the end of the canyon, and while she waited by some wild roses for her mother to catch up, I climbed the rocks to a flat area where little stacks of rocks marked other visitors' journeys.

I collected my own rocks along with my thoughts and, with prayers of gratitude and surrender, stacked them in recognition of my climbing achievement and in honor of this sacred vortex. I sat in the silence of this place, listening to the wind in the cottonwood trees and the occasional rock tumble down the cliff. I could "feel" the canyon here, in the quiet stillness of nature.

My young companion's mother joined me and stacked her own little pile of rocks. In the graying light, we walked out of that canyon together as her daughter jogged on ahead. Much to my surprise, the sun was shining brightly, and it was warm when I got back to my car, a reminder of the way that light, dark and temperature play differently in various environments. I headed over to Devil's Bridge, a moderate hike that only called for about another thirty minutes of hiking. Snacking on raw almonds and an apple, I checked this hike off my list, getting close enough to see the beautiful rock formation as the last hiker ahead of me made her way down to the place where I had stopped. She pointed it out to me. Close enough, I figured, and asked if I might walk out with her in the now fading daylight.

I capped my weekend off with another hike, one with a personal guide – a wonderful young man around twenty who had come to Sedona from South America to work for the summer. We hiked up the old Flagstaff Road to an outcropping of rocks that overlooked the town. I could see the white buildings of the airport on the mesa across the valley. It stuck out like a sore thumb, a white lump on the blazing red rocks. My guide pointed out Eagle Rock, a natural sculpture of an eagle's head protruding from the side of the mountain. He encouraged me to walk out onto the cliffs to get a better view. Once I was comfortable on the cliffs, he stepped back and left me alone with the rocks and the mountains. I watched the eye of the eagle watch the city below. I stared until it disappeared into the rocky face of the cliff, and then I listened...

In the magic of silence, they called me: the drums, echoing up out of the distant void. Echoing the heartbeat of the canyon, the drums sang to me of ceremony danced long ago, below these sacred rocks, under the watchful eye of an eagle. In the silence of listening, I found the magic. Is silence the key to finding me, to getting off my shelf?

The return trip to Clovis left me with hours to ponder the weekend, to journal the magical experiences and chronicle my discoveries. It felt like the downward spiral out of me, the one that was ballooning me onto that shelf, must surely be metabolic. My system must be out of whack – makes sense when you eat cookies for comfort.

I had weaned myself off the feel-better meds, all the while wondering why I had such an aversion to drugs designed to help me be more balanced. Was it a psychological block, and if so, who put it there? At the time I started them, I was seeing a psychologist to try to get my own "toolbox" open once again; I was struggling to find the key. I'd thought I only needed to get past all the physical and emotional losses of the past few years, but then I heard my mother's voice whispering in my ear: "You've got to pull yourself up by your own bootstraps and get going. It's all up to you, you know!"

That sneaky little inherited belief, buried deep within me, had me convinced that I must do it all and do it on my own. After all, it is ALL up to me; everything is my responsibility. Polish off that top shelf, I need to climb higher.

Through all the death and drama, my daughter Raney was concerned and loving, bound and determined to hold me in balance. She stepped into the role of caretaker for her father and me. Her dad welcomed this. I struggled with it all. (I'm supposed to do it all.)

Though I didn't welcome the smothering, I totally understood it. I knew it wasn't fair to let her take on such a massive responsibility, I knew I needed to take care of us, so why couldn't I say no? It was easier to do nothing, say nothing and just sit in that overstuffed chair until the day finally came when I couldn't.

I moved away from the co-dependent expert I had become and began to regain my own sense of self. As mother and daughter, were we destined to butt heads off and on? I struggled to find the way to communicate all of this. If there was one thing she was good at, it was telling it like it is. I needed to take that kind of communication to heart and learn to speak my truth in a way that was 'safe' for both of us.

We were driving home from town late one afternoon. As she turned onto the freeway, I looked over at her, at the beautiful and strong woman she had become. So full of love.

"Honey," I said, "I can't do this anymore. You have to leave me alone for a while, let me move through this on my own, to figure out who I am and who I am becoming."

With those words, I pushed the reset button on what was to be yet another climb back into me and a slow descent off the shelf.

The best way for me to find my way back to me was to make something, write something, teach something – in other words, JUST DO SOMETHING! It is in the planning, the designing, and then the crafting of an idea that I am brought back to that place that for me, fuels my joy and ignites my soul's fire. Creativity in any form makes me happy. Like the song says, "Sunshine nearly always makes me smile..." I'd change it up a bit and sing, "Creativity always makes me smile."

A Way Off the Shelf: Morning Dance

I use this exercise to bring myself present, to honor and call in the strength and beauty of the Elementals to support me throughout my day. It fills me with their warmth and the blessings of Mother Earth and Father Sky/Sun.

In doing this, I can move my own loving energy out into the world to begin each new day with my eyes, mind, and heart wide open – aware, awake, and with intentionality.

You begin by standing (barefoot if you can) with your feet spread shoulder-width apart, your knees slightly bent. Put the palms of your hands together in a prayer position over your heart, inhaling the fragrance of the morning air and gently bowing in gratitude for this new day. Allow yourself to "feel" the loving support of The Mother and open yourself and your body to receive her gifts and the gifts of the Sun and the Sky Fathers.

When you are ready, gently open your arms, extending them in a circular fashion out and down as you bend over, scooping up the energy of Mother Earth. Hand over hand, alternating the movements of your arms, gently pull the renewing energy of Mother Earth up into your body. Remain in this slightly stooped position and repeat this movement, scooping up and pulling into your center, the loving, renewing and grounding energy of the Earth. Hold it for a moment at your power center (that place just below your navel, perhaps between your second and third chakras). This is the place of your body-mind, your instinctual center.

As you feel your center fill up, stand taller and begin using your hands to move this beautiful energy up from your power center, gently pushing this energy up your torso and into your heart. Hold it there briefly.

Inhale another deep breath of gratitude and exhale anything you sense might keep your heart closed today. Inhale all possibilities and exhale all limitations.

As you feel called to continue, move this Earth energy on up through your chest, your throat, your head and opening your crown chakra. Allow your own body to open to the morning light and to the heavens above.

Spreading your arms wide, lean slightly back and tilt your face up to feel the warmth of the sun on your face – feel it relax your throat so you may speak only your truth this day. Let it open your heart to love and only love as you prepare for your day. Inhale this universal light and "see" it fill your power center, releasing any disease or stress that you may be clinging to. Breathe in the beauty all around you, and as you exhale let go of any tension you may feel in your body. Draw in all the radiance of the morning sun to "light" you up on this new day.

Relaxing this open stance, let your arms drop gently to your sides and just stand easily for a moment, facing the morning light that is filled with all possibility as it illuminates your entire being and breathe... take a moment and just listen.

Sway with the movement of the air around you and listen to the whispers on the wind for the day's divine inspiration and guidance. Breathe...

When you are ready, lift your arms up as though reaching for the light and bring them up over your head; cup this radiance and begin to pull it down into your body.

Feel it fill your head, clearing your thoughts of all negativity and judgment as it opens the pathways to your own knowing and all there is for you to learn in this new day.

The warmth of the morning light opens your ears to hearing unconditionally, the truth of all others. Continue to pull this universal light down into your body, into your heart, your chest and inhale, filling your lungs with the fresh air of this new morning's first breath.

Using your hands, cup this radiant, universal divine energy around your sacred center, opening to your daily dreaming and to each little death and rebirth that will transform this day. Honor your movement with gratitude for each lesson learned, and continue to push this radiant, grateful, love-filled light down into Mother Earth as you bend over, releasing all that has moved through you to her, for her to absorb and transform.

Reach all the way down to the Earth, touching her. Placing your hand(s) on the ground, you are the conduit connecting Heaven and Earth with your gratitude for this new morning, for the fading darkness and the rising light, for all the beings who live on, above and within this magnificent planet.

Standing tall once again, head tilted slightly back, bring your open arms in a circular fashion together above your heads, palms together closing the circle. Keeping your palms together, bring them back down to your chest. Resting over your heart, offer whatever prayers, affirmations, and inspirations you are called to speak. Inhale this new day, set your intentions for new beginnings, for your love, light, and truth to be with you on this day's earth walk.

Exhale your love for all the Beings of Light and Love that

surround and support you as you move your hands out, palms facing the world, pushing the love and beauty of YOU out into the world.

Take a few moments and dance with the sun, sway with the wind and listen to the morning songs from the trees, the birds and all the beings that have joined you in this celebration of a new day. Aho!

If you feel drawn to continue, simply repeat these movements in whatever way you are guided. Play with the morning light and enjoy your day.

Chapter Two

FALLING APART

*Spirit sings through unknown things into open ears unclogged
from everyday routines. They hear in the silence the long,
lost messages left between hidden worlds.*

rofessionally speaking, the year 2010 was my best ever. In 2011 things overall seemed to turn around, to get better for me; momentum returned. I was working, growing, and creating abundance, moving with positivity and passion, teaching. Slowly but steadily, I lost excess weight, the right way, one conscious bite at a time as I began to move again, to walk farther and with more strength in each step. But at the end of this year, with the holidays and all that comes with them, the heaviness returned – the grief, the sadness, the disconnection (Ryan's birthday was December 4). Who wants a Christmas tree anyway? Not me, not Danny, not really, but we do have a grandson to think about. I'll have to put it up and decorate it, just me, by myself, lonely. Why bother? I'll have hot chocolate and a cookie, please. Better yet, I'll bake cookies and make candy and pretend it's all okay.

I watched the pounds creeping back with another knee surgery in December – what's that make, five now, each fix lasting for a shorter period of time. Doc wants to replace the knee altogether, and I'm almost ready... almost. Weeks of recovery follow, and physical therapy isn't enough to keep me out of my overstuffed chair stuffing many, too many, cookies for comfort. Emotional pain killers they were. I could eat an entire box of See's candy as the downhill slide got steeper.

Five, ten pounds and oh, okay, back off the cookies. Traveling, eating poorly, portion sizes growing, late-night cravings fulfilled and bam! – I was once again heading down the slippery slope. In trying to stop the slide, I jumped into a diet program unprepared to be part of a group with accountability and support. I had lost self-control and was not accepting responsibility for any of it and, did I mention, having to follow "rules" drives me crazy? Did I also mention that budgets of any kind, restrictions, drive me crazy too? Budgeting points, calories, ounces – yuck! So, like diving into any venture without enough preparation or training, the difficulties multiplied. I lost self-control and just let go.

Weight has been a constant struggle since my first pregnancy, when I gained sixty pounds and stopped so much of the activity that kept me burning calories. My added weight was a source of discomfort for not just myself, but for my mother as well. About a year after Ryan was born, she volunteered to babysit one day a week if I would attend a TOPS (Take Off Pounds Sensibly) meeting and work on losing my baby weight. And it worked. I lost the most weight out of anyone in my local chapter, was crowned "queen" for the year, and given the opportunity to attend the regional convention, all expenses paid.

The convention would be the following February (I think it was mid-year when chapter awards are given). As fate would have it, I got pregnant with our daughter and like with my first pregnancy, the pounds piled back on. In fact, I gained more that the allotted two pounds per month for a pregnancy, specified in the TOPS guidelines, lost my crown before the convention, and someone else was sent in my place. I never went back after the baby was born. As time passed, I figured out how to lose most of the weight and got back down into a manage-able size; at least I could ride a horse again, fit my seat in the saddle.

My mother was five-foot-seven, and when she married my father had a twenty-inch waist (there was little hope I would wear her wedding dress). In photos taken during my childhood, she had that same narrow waist. My sister, who had always been thin, had a baby many years later and only gained sixteen pounds with her pregnancy. I'm sure that made Mom proud until my sister Pam's waistline began to expand as the years went by. I remember Mom commenting on how she didn't understand how her daughters let their weight get out of control. I asked her how she managed not to, and her answer was that if the other women in the groups she belonged to could keep their weight down, so could she. Fast food wasn't on the menu until my high school years. Perhaps that was one of her saving graces.

I was wearing white pants one day when we were together and she commented, "How nice you look today but think how much thinner you might look in darker pants."

Words are so powerful. I didn't hear the compliment; I just heard the "but" and all that followed. I felt her disappointment. My weight seemed to be a constant source of frustration for Mom. On the other hand, given her own belief that "thinner would be better," it may just have been her wish for me. Those words spoken were seeding food for thought or, perhaps, just planting weeds that would later need pulling.

I really hated the "responsibility" of it all. Cookies eased the guilt, my body blew up like a balloon, fat was loaded on. I gained more and more weight on speed dial and loved the journey, the satisfaction of food. My body did not, and it showed. There I was nearly a year later, with all the weight back.

I had to identify with a plan. I had to consciously work to rid myself of lethargy and my own lack of initiative to move. However, there were consequences to my ride down the slippery slope: lower back problems were exacerbated, knee pain grew intense, and respiratory issues resurfaced for the fourth time in two years. I was losing the battle, again, for a strong and healthy body.

Fast forward to the fall, and the impending birth of my second grandbaby.

For me, this new baby meant it was more important than ever for me to be present, to be able to move, to find a way and a reason to get up, to get off the damned shelf. Fear snuck in between the cracks of expectant joy as I remembered how hard it was when the first one was born. All those uneasy conversations, untrusting confrontations, rules, and regulations. Was I really being called to float down this arduous river in my "poor me" canoe, again? Was it time to bail out and swim for the shore?

It was, I knew it… how else would I ever get anywhere else, be any different, do anything more? It was important that I find me again so I can be present for my grandchildren and not escape into candy bars and cookies. I wanted to be the mother and grandmother I envisioned with joy and grace. I would be without regret, it was time to dream the me I wanted to be and not the one I thought I was supposed to be.

The vision-questing thing was scary. It was the unknown part of the evolution process in pursuit of my vision that had me stuck in "no-decision" territory. That baby would come and life will go on. It was up to me to decide how that would look for me and how it would be for them.

Dreaming me, I sat in silence with these thoughts that had come to me during a past visit to Mt. Shasta. I was floundering about in all the possibilities of being ME. I could see there was a path. Which way do I go? What would tomorrow look like, feel like, be like as the me I would be, or rather as the me I wanted to be?

In that silence, back on that mountain, these words were gifted to me on the wind: *"Reclaim the voice of your truth and understand the inherent personal movement that is involved in this reclamation."*

Now I saw it, the dream, my Quest – Reclaiming Me. In re-discovering my life's passion, that which brings such joy to me and to those around me, I connected with my joy. I connected with that contagion that spreads the energy of joy. I served no one, least of all me, when I hung out in misery with "poor cow."

The rest of this process of evolving I leave to Spirit and let the answers to great unhappiness and emotional distress come from my God and my "council" in whatever form those answers come. My dreaming has returned. Although still confusing and sometimes weird, at least the consciousness of a dream is back.

Today is the tomorrow I dreamed about yesterday.

Oh, yeah, that's right! I must dream it.

There may be a key in that thought... I remember, I have a dream.

17

A Way Off the Shelf: "Stalking your Dream"

STEP INTO THE MYSTERY…

"If you speak to a person who is standing in a powerless position and tell her to take her power, she becomes frightened because you are implying change. She must take a step into the mystery of the unknown to become powerful."
–Lynn Andrews

The following is my adaptation of an exercise I learned in
The Lynn Andrews Mystery School

Have a comfortable spot picked out for yourself with a journal and pen handy. You will either visualize yourself in a sacred circle or perhaps you can create one for yourself, inside or out. It is easily done with your intent alone, but it is always nice to use four small stones (or more if you like) to set the cardinal directions, North, South, East and West. Allow yourself enough space to sit within your circle and be able to turn about to face each of these directions.

Many traditions have their ways of creating a sacred circle; you make that decision for yourself, there are no rules here. I was taught to enter in the East and begin my journey in the South, moving in a clockwise direction to the West and the North and in the East, circling into the center, testing the air, the wind, and the magic within the mystery that holds my answers. Open yourself to your own divine guidance and pay close attention to all the messages waiting for you in this journey, be they words, sounds, symbols or colors.

This time in our world is new, and it is different. It holds a very raw and unknown energetic as all the old ways are falling aside, dissolving, or being pulled apart. Release your expectations along with the old, perhaps difficult, and rigid ways. Let yourself move into all the possibilities of what is new, growing, and being birthed in our world today.

Take your journal and pen and lay them close by you or in your lap as you settle into a comfortable position and take a few deep breaths. The process of journaling your journey as you move in and out of first and second attention, may be new for some of you. Let yourself go with it. You are going to stalk, to pursue, chase, go in search of your dream around this sacred circle in a dreamlike journey. As you complete your time in each direction, you will come back into the present moment and briefly journal your experience taking note of any messages, symbols, shapes, or colors that you receive. Allow the energy of your new dream to begin to find you.

Each of your dreams will have a life of its own — its own vibrational frequency, its own color and shape. As with the creation of anything, there is a giveaway somewhere along the way — when great art is created, forms change; the paint leaves its tube and is transformed into a magnificent painting. Today you are going to stalk your dream, see where you need to transform the old and bring in the new.

Take a few more relaxing breaths. See or sense your sacred circle surrounded now by your guides and guardians, angels and ancestors, allies and any helping spirits that benevolently show up to support you as you stalk your dream with the four directions. Pay attention as you move around this wheel, your sacred circle. Perhaps a new guide or helping spirit will step forward to walk with you through your dreams journey.

See yourself now, sitting in the center of your circle... consciously bring yourself present and to this place; take another deep cleansing breath and begin to think about your dream or your goals, your vision for tomorrow and the future... perhaps you will speak an opening prayer for this sacred journey and when you are ready...

READ the following: Allow yourself to move into the space between the words. Let yourself forget about your body as best you can now and move into the dream... look to the South on your circle. That represents the physical aspects of your life, the substance of your body and the Earth we sit upon. It is in the South that the physical manifestation of your dream takes place. It is with trust and innocence that you look at your dream. Stay conscious of this place of the child and bring an aspect of joyfulness and play into your dream...

- Where do you sense your dream resides in your body?

- How do you see your dream physically?

- How will you physically experience your dream?

Look around your circle once again and let your gaze soften as it comes to rest on the guardian standing in your South direction.

What are they holding?

Is it a symbol or color?

Is it an animal or bird, maybe it is a word?

Look closely...

What message does this South guardian have for you and your dream? ... What do you need to let go of here in the South to manifest your dream for this year? ... What do you physically need to do in this next year to make your dream come true? ...Take some time and communicate with this sacred being.

After you have read through the above, close your eyes and "see" yourself in the center of your sacred circle facing the direction of the South. Ask your questions. See the Guardian across from your and spend some time here stalking your dream in the energy of the South.

When you are ready, pick up your journal and make a few notes about what you have seen, sensed, or heard.

When you are finished...

READ the following and allow yourself to settle back into the center of your sacred circle. Turn and bring your attention now to the West direction, the home of the Great Dreaming Bear who carries your sacred dream. This is a place of death and of rebirth, a place of transformation. Here is where you will connect with the emotional aspects of your dream.

- Can you touch the feeling of the dream?

- When you contemplate your dream, what emotions do you feel?

- Are you afraid to dream?

- Are you afraid of what it will mean to achieve your dream?

- Can you see the transformation of your dream into reality as you look ahead?

Look around your circle once again and let your gaze come to rest on the guardian standing in your West direction.

What are they holding?

Is it a symbol or color?

Is it an animal or bird, maybe it is a word?

Look closely…

What message does this West guardian have for you and your dream?

What feelings do you need to let go of here in the West to manifest your dream for this year?

What do you emotionally need to do in this next year to make your dream come true?

Take some time and communicate with this sacred being.

After you have read through the above, close your eyes and "see" yourself in your sacred circle facing the direction of the West. Ask your questions. See the Guardian across from you and spend some time here stalking your dream in the energy of the West.

When you are ready, pick up your journal and make a few notes about what you have seen, sensed, or heard from the West.

When you are finished…

READ the following and allow yourself to settle back into the center of your sacred circle. Taking another deep breath, turn and bring your attention to the North direction, the place of the Great White Buffalo and the place of Spirit in your dream. This is the place of strength and wisdom, the place of prayer.

- Will you bring Spirit, your God/Goddess/Creator into your dream quest?

- Do you seek inspiration along your journeys?

- Do you celebrate your progress with gratitude and joy, giving thanks for the good and honoring the gifts of the struggle when things are not so good?

Look to the North of your circle once again and look into the eyes of the Guardian standing in this North direction.

What are they holding?

Is it a symbol or color?

Is it an animal or bird, maybe it is a word? Look closely…

What message does this North guardian have for you and your dream?

What do you need to let go of here in the North to manifest your dream in the coming months?

What will you be inspired to do in this next year to make your dream come true?

Take some time and communicate with this sacred being.

After you have read through the above, close your eyes and "see" yourself in your sacred circle facing the direction of the North. Ask your questions. See the Guardian and spend some time here, stalking your dream in the energy of the North.

When you are ready, pick up your journal and make a few notes about what you have seen, sensed, or heard in the North of your circle.

Write a short prayer to the Spirit Keeper of your dream asking this luminous being to be ever present and available for you to work with, throughout your dream journey.

When you are finished…

READ the following and allow yourself to settle comfortably back in the center of your sacred circle. Taking another deep breath, turn to face the next direction and bring your attention to the East, to the place of the Magnificent Eagle who flies highest of all, seeing the greater picture and all its pieces. This is the place of the Old Wise One who watches over you and guides you on your path. It is the place of the rising Sun, and it is the place where you test all your previous commitments and ideals for their truth in your life with this new dream.

- Can you hold the image of your dream throughout the year, seeing always the bigger picture?

- Will you let your mind sabotage the experience of your dream as you analyze it to death?

- Will you trust this dream and ride into your battle to claim it as the heyoka warrior would, mounted on your horse backwards carrying a broken lance? This is the action of ultimate trust in you and your journey.

Look around your circle once again and let your gaze connect with the guardian standing in your East direction.

What are they holding?

Is it a symbol or color, a shape?

Is it an animal or bird, maybe it is just a word? Look closely…

What message does this East guardian have for you and your dream?

What do you mentally need to let go of here in the East to manifest your dream for this year?

Where are you overanalyzing this journey?

Can you really place your trust in this process and know that the outcome is exactly what it is supposed to be, and take the journey into your dream, releasing your expectations of the final outcome?

What new ideas do you need to bring into your life to manifest your dream?

Take some time and communicate with this sacred being.

When you are ready, come back again now more fully present in your sacred circle. Make your notes about this visit with the East direction.

<u>**After you have read through the above, close your eyes**</u> and "see" yourself in your sacred circle facing the direction of the East. Ask your questions. See the Guardian there and spend some time stalking your dream in the energy of the East.

As you finish, bring yourself now fully present in your space, in your circle, here and NOW! Continue to journal the information you received in the East and any other images, messages, sounds, or colors you may remember as you SEE your dream taking shape.

<u>**When you are ready, move into your Art Space**</u> and paint your dream...

Pick out the colors for the "vision" of your dream using the information you received in the meditation. Take your paper and a tea light candle, some paint brushes, and a small plastic container. Fill the bowl with some water and use the lid as your paint palette. Finding a place to paint, set up your space with your candle at the top of your art paper and when you are ready, light it and silently call in your muses to be with you in this adventure, acknowledge them and ....

LET THE FUN BEGIN and paint your dream!

Chapter Three

FIRST TIME ON THE SHELF

"I recognized ME in a flash of lightning,

before the shadows descended again…

And in that instant, I recognized hope."

I understood freedom at an early age. It was cultivated at the private elementary school I attended – one classroom for each grade level. It was a "lab school," part of Fresno State University. Teachers were trained there, and kids were free there. Nobody told me not to swing on the maypole although the nurse did get tired of bandaging my skinned knees. We didn't get grades – we either passed or we didn't. I didn't feel stuffed into a box or judged for being outside of one. It was an empowering way to learn.

That freedom would go away, get lost in the rules of public school and society's "norms." It would be, perhaps, my first introduction to loss and grief – even my first trip to the proverbial "shelf" where I mastered setting myself aside.

Life circumstances changed for my family in the summer between second and third grades. My dad's business partner ran off with their payroll and bankrupted their company. My stay-at-home, coiffed, and aproned mom, who polished our shoes when we took naps, would have to go to work. My out-of-the Army, previously self-employed Dad couldn't find a job. He wouldn't go after the partner for the money and sank into a deep depression. I just remember he slept a lot on the weekends, especially when his back "was out."

My parents tried car-pooling, sharing with us that the bus program had been canceled. It didn't work out, so midyear my sister and I transferred from the private lab school at the University to the public elementary school in our neighborhood.

There I was, planted in a strange room with no familiar faces and a whole new set of expectations I wasn't even aware of. I was eight and a half years old, in the middle of the third grade, wearing poodle skirts and pink sparkly glasses. How do you hang from the monkey bars in a skirt or slide into home plate? You don't! Girls/little ladies didn't do such things; those were the games of boys. No friends, no soccer (it was not heard of in public school), sit still, pay attention and for heaven's sake, stop talking so much.

My world changed overnight! Suddenly there were different rules for girls and boys – it was the 1950s and the freedom/ openness I had taken for granted at the lab school was unknown in the public education system. No one had ever yelled at me for chasing Eric around the playground at Fresno State. He was the only one who could outrun me. Now I was being told that girls couldn't play football with the boys at recess. So what if I skinned my knees a lot? That's what band-aids were invented for.

Then there was Old Lady Matsel in the fifth grade. She sent me to the principal's office for standing up to the boys in a baseball game. No more baseball at recess for Vicki. At least it was still alright for girls to ride bicycles. Climbing trees, not so much, but we had a great mulberry tree in our backyard where I could hang out in the branches, see far and high, get a different view on life. I didn't understand the sadness that was creeping into my heart one "No, girls don't do that" at a time.

The school music director offered us the stringed instruments like violins (my sister played) and the woodwinds, but percussion and brass were left to the boys (perhaps the adults thought them too heavy for a girl). I played the clarinet. I loved marching, the tempo, the beat.

Later, high school band would give me the opportunity to march when ROTC was still just for the boys. The sound of a timpani drum touched something deep inside that I didn't recognize at the time as anything more than the bass held in music. I think it touched my heart.

My mother had been in a drum and bugle corps when she was in high school. I have her drumsticks.

Music was part of my life at home too. I got a used guitar for my tenth birthday and the next Christmas, Santa gifted me with lessons so I could play it.

As the sadness deepened with each new discovery of girl's don't or can't, I got busier with being a girl. I learned to play the piano at twelve and used it as my mood meter. I could play melancholy and I could play happy. I could impress a boy walking up to the door for a date. Of course, being five-foot-ten at fourteen didn't make dating easy. I was so self-conscious about being taller than the boys. I stayed busy, with band, the girls' athletic association (we could play intermural volleyball and basketball after school). Swimming and tennis were the only NCAA-sanctioned sports for girls back then, so I was on the diving team. Title IX was a decade away. I filled my spare time and summer days being active in the Masonic organization Job's Daughters, as a craft teacher at recreation centers, and as a camp counselor at Sequoia Lake.

Gangly and taller than the boys, I was a charm school candidate in junior high school. I would learn how to walk properly, speak properly, sit, and stand properly. I would learn to float up the stairs so the book on my head wouldn't fall off. Who wrote that damned book of etiquette anyway? None of it fit me. I wanted to run up those stairs and slide down the banister.

Years later, Mom told me that the only thing that saved my jeans from the garbage can was the fact that when she could get me into a dress I would primp in front of the mirror. I loved the freedom of pants. I climbed trees, rode the swings sideways as my horse and raced bicycles around the block. *You* try riding full-speed ahead, keeping your knees together while wearing a skirt on a bicycle.

My mother's mother never wore pants; it wasn't ladylike. That was the point of view my mother lived with, although she did allow herself the comfort of slacks and shorts. Hard to take a trip to the lake for a boat ride in a dress. It wasn't until the polyester leisure suits hit the scene in the seventies that my very proper grandmother decided that it was now "OK" for her to wear pants.

The message I was getting during all those growing up years was to stop being who I was. They were telling me not to express what fueled my joy. I was to be ladylike and silent. I wanted to run, jump, play out loud and outside, not sit demurely in a corner with a doll or a cup of tea. The footstool in front of the couch became a horse for me as I rode the trails with Davy Crockett and Hopalong Cassidy.

I learned incredibly young that "doing" busy kept the emotions at bay. I could be a productive, valued member of society, all the while putting myself – me – right up there on a shelf.

I stayed up late and slept half the day away on weekends. Sleep was another way to keep "me" at bay, working hard to be what I thought everyone wanted me to be. Holding back any part of myself kept me glued to that shelf. "Stay busy" was my unconscious directive with Brownie scouts, Girl Scouts, tri-gray Y, and summer camp, music and swimming lessons and of course there was "charm" school at thirteen. My mom believed that keeping busy was the way you stayed out of trouble. Summer school and VolunTeen programs every summer allowed her to work without need of a babysitter.

Dad was selling cars by now; I'm junior high age. Sales was the perfect gig for him. He was very likeable, made friends easily. His six-foot-six stature drew people's attention and his easy way of being put them at ease. I inherited his gift of gab and salesmanship.

Sometimes he would drop me at school; other times I rode my bike or walked. There were always little chores for us that Mom expected to be done when she got home. The dusting, vacuuming, emptying the dishwasher, and folding the clothes were the busywork that filled that time between school or afterschool programs and Mom getting home from work.

My mother was organized, a planner, keeper of the calendar and "the books," so to speak. She was up ahead of everyone else each morning, dressed, makeup on, her dark brown hair perfectly coiffed.

I remember her sleeping with folded toilet paper wrapped around her "updo" with everything bobby-pinned into place when she went to bed. She would be ready for her day and look "good" doing it. Her routine was to run the dishwasher before bed, along with a load of laundry. In the morning, she would have us empty the dishwasher and put the clothes in the dryer while she made breakfast. Dad would be reading the paper in his morning place. He made breakfast on Sundays.

Mom had a plan, and she worked her plan. If the other ladies she knew could stay thin, by God, she could too and would, her entire life. Indeed, she never broke one hundred and fifty pounds. I took it all in, though as mentioned I didn't learn the weight part very well. And I have always laughed at being organizationally challenged but well accomplished in getting everything I needed to get done, done anyway.

What my mom didn't teach me was that it was okay to be "me." Instead, the lesson I got was to put on a mask for every aspect of my life that didn't fit the girl mold. "What will people think?" she would ask. "Your actions are a direct reflection on your family," she preached. No pressure there! Get caught stealing penny candy and OMG, what will people think of your parents?

I started "buying" people into my life that year we changed schools, like stealing candy to give away. It became a lifelong habit. Not the stealing, *please*. Buying people into my life (by giving to and doing for them), was a way for me to be "of service" and to be honest, looking back, it gave me a sense of what I will call here, power. It felt good.

I always worried about my mother finding out what I was up to – she seemed to have eyes everywhere and knew people who knew me everywhere I went; and I felt guilty whenever I strayed from "her rules for ladies," seen or not. It wasn't that I stepped outside the lines often. I was a "good kid," and did everything I thought I needed to do to be seen as such. What my mom thought mattered.

I *really* didn't want to disappoint my dad. I wanted to be the young lady he expected me to be, but it was hard when I'd rather play baseball or rope a steer. He tried to buy me a new dress for Christmas every year in my twenties. I used to tease him and ask, "Why? Where would I wear it, to a roping?" By then, I was totally involved in the horse world I loved and lived in jeans and boots.

Daddy was always there, but I sense now that "he" wasn't really "there." I would learn decades later that he suffered from depression, which explained a lot. I recognize that energy of "not here" that I can move into myself if I am not careful, disconnecting while still being present.

It's funny, I can vividly remember telling my mom not to tell daddy when I admitted to her that my boyfriend and I had played around. Daddy had told me a story about how much he cared for a girl when he was young. He dropped out of school in the ninth grade to work and he was, from what I understand, a bit of a bad boy. He got a little drunk and asked this girl out to "party." After that night together, he never saw her again. That was our sex talk — don't before marriage or the boys will lose all respect for you and find a "good" girl to marry. I cried the first time I made love to my future husband, all the fear of "now he will leave" streaming into what should have been a beautiful beginning to "us." I wasn't afraid to love Danny, I was just afraid he would lose respect for me and move on since there was no reason to buy the cow when the milk was free. I think that's how Dad put it.

He was a very protective father as well, though on the surface, he rarely showed it. I remember one time going with him and Mom to the bowling alley. My older sister Pam was already there and they were checking up on her. We sat at one end of the lanes and Dad watched as Pam bowled with some friends. There were some guys hanging around with them. When they were finished bowling, Pam and her friend left, and we all followed. Apparently, Dad had noticed a couple of the young men in t-shirts and jeans walk out behind her. Sure enough, Pam got in her car, the boys got in theirs and followed. Well, Dad zoomed out of that parking lot and cut those guys off. They pulled over to the curb while my sister, oblivious to what was going on behind her, drove on. Dad, all six-foot-six of him, got out of the car, walked around to the back of it, laid his glasses on the trunk and had a conversation with those two young men. It was short and sweet. Those boys got back in their car and left in a different direction than the way my sister's car had gone. Dad slid back into the driver's seat and we headed for home. Nothing was ever said about it really, just a few giggles at what might have been going through those boys' minds when confronted by our dad.

He was there. Then again, I don't remember ever having an adult-to-adult conversation with my dad. My busyness kept me from spending time with him in those teenage and young adult years when I might have been asking questions or sharing stories, learning about him, who he was and where he came from. My sister has more stories about Dad; she and Mom didn't get along and Dad was her go-to for talk time. I on the other hand, spent a lot of time with Mom, she even traveled with me on some of my business ventures. Mom would talk around subjects but never reveal much detail about her past or her growing-up years. Knowing what I do now about energy, and looking back on what I was feeling then, I realize Mom was angry about her childhood. When I asked her what her favorite toy growing up was, she answered, "I didn't have time to play, I had to take care of Richard" – her younger brother by five years.

Though I know now, *when* I started "buying" people into my life, I still haven't uncovered, pinpointed or explored why I felt the need to do so. I can only assume that the changes in school, home, stability, and "energy" in my life threw me out of myself and into an addictive behavior of exiting the scene in favor of shelf life.

I didn't understand the dynamics of energy and power back then, but I did understand what it felt like when someone liked me because I could give them things or do things for them. This was codependency, and it was like a drug I would try to wean myself off my whole life.

Understanding energy is a lifelong journey. Nature is a wonderful schoolhouse for seeing and feeling it, for connecting with and understanding how you interact with different energies. Sit with a tree and listen. Relax by a stream or bubbling brook and watch the light play on the water. How do you feel? How are they different?

When you meet people, "see" them as that tree or stream, a rock or a cloud, the moon, or the sun. How do they "feel"? How do you feel around them? When your energetics match, you will connect naturally. When there is some resistance, check it out. When there is a "push-back," like when you hold the positive ends of two magnets together and they repel each other, look well about it and consider whether the work it takes to stay connected is worth the effort and energy. Perhaps that person is just a short-term teacher for you, not a lifetime friend.

When I feel disconnected from my people, my home, my place with me, I look to nature for encouragement and inspiration. It has become one of my most powerful ways to get off the shelf.

A Way Off the Shelf: Conversation with a Rock

This is a wonderful way to get out of your head and into your heart space, to listen with your body-mind to the wisdom of the ancient Stone People.

Wander outside a bit and listen for a small rock to call your attention to it.

Pick it up and ask it if it has a message for you, or if it just wants to be admired and moved about the yard or park or wherever you are. If the rock indicates that it does have a message for you, find a place to sit with it, even bring it back inside with you.

If you are familiar with smudging (using sage or other herbs to create smoke), gently cleanse and clear this stone teacher so that it may be easily heard. Take the time to smudge yourself as well, so that you may clearly receive the message it has to share. If smoke is not an option for you, you can most certainly use a feather, even a small branch of leaves. It isn't about the tool you use; it is all about your intent for the process to cleanse and clear the way for you and this stone teacher to share a conversation.

Have paper and a pen or pencil with you and sit with this rock in a place of quiet stillness. Open your heart to listen. Ask this slow and quiet one: What belief you have inherited from your family that no longer serves you? Be still and listen...

You may recognize one belief (a paradigm), or perhaps you discover more than one limiting belief that you are ready to acknowledge and let go. As they come up for you, write them down. Record any messages you may receive about how they have affected your decisions and actions, how these limiting beliefs may have limited your life.

When you are ready, when you have written it/them down on your paper, you are ready to release them. Visualize these inherited or limiting beliefs and the feelings that are attached to them going to a place in nature where the earth can transform them into beauty.

Take your notes and your helping spirit stone back outside with you or if you are still outdoors, ask the teacher of this stone to direct you to where the rock wants to be placed back on the earth.

When you have found that place, take a few moments to speak aloud those limiting beliefs, those old paradigms that no longer serve who you are today. When you are finished, place your folded-up paper under the stone and return it to the ground it has chosen with you. Speak your prayers and gratitude to this rock for the service it has offered to you on this special day.

Allow yourself just a few more minutes and breathe in the fresh air. As you do, inhale the beauty that surrounds you and allow it to fill the void that has been left by the exit of these old belief structures. Exhale any residual thoughts or feelings as they come up and continue this breathing until you are complete with your ceremony. You might even place a bit of tobacco or cornmeal on the ground where the stone began its journey with you and where it ended if these places are different. If you don't have anything handy, you can always pull a strand of your own hair in gratitude or even spit (the earth loves moisture), giving thanks for your time and this space and the stone.

Chapter Four

BE SEEN AND NOT HEARD

I just realized I am on a quiet street

in a small country town.

Few people are around.

Not too sure how I got here.

Have I been asleep that long?

Things feel slow, I'm drawn to all

that isn't going on around me.

Where are the cars, the throngs of people

Pushing and shoving their way down sidewalks?

The trucks and bicycles? I hear a dog bark.

A shaggy mutt, big, brown-eyed cutie staring back at me…

My mind wanders to where I am, how I got here.

What is the last thing I remember?

Oh yeah! "Vicki, be still, the adults are trying to talk."

on't tell me to be quiet! a voice inside me screamed. I was sitting with my husband Danny at the Peacock Coffee Shop, the local watering hole where horse

39

folks came on the weekends to shoot the bull and relish Grandma Glynnis' country cookin'.

"I already know what you know," Danny said after shushing me, "I want to know what *they* (his coffee shop compadres) know." Basically, he was telling me to be seen and not heard. This is painful for anyone, but perhaps even more so for a storyteller, as this is the way we connect with people.

I never went back to that coffee shop with him. It had gone from a fun place to hang out to just another reminder that "Vicki talks too much." I was, in essence, being shown the shelf.

The first person who said this about me was a teacher. She told my mother who then relayed the message to me. She told my mother she wished I didn't talk so much, adding, "The problem is, she's usually right. She's always the first to raise her hand and offer an answer to whatever I ask, and sometimes before I ask it." Mother didn't tell me *that* part until years later. Looking back, I think she thought it would have given me permission to continue talking and back then, children were to be seen and not heard.

I remember visiting my grandparents in Missouri. Grandma and Grandpa played cards every week at different friends' homes. My sister and I went along and were given a quilt to spread out on the floor and cards of our own to play with; we also always had a book with us. That was "our space." We were told we'd earn a nickel or a dime if we stayed on that blanket and played *quietly* until our grandparents were ready to leave. Quiet being the operative word here; be quiet was the message I heard.

Growing up came with labels. If you talked too much in class, raised your hand all the time, or volunteered for tasks, you got labeled "Teachers Pet." When you always had the answers, you were a "Know-It-All." The brutal truth of these obvious yet subliminal messages didn't sink in until as an adult, I was shut down completely with the "be here but be quiet" in that coffee shop.

These days, I am still very conscious of when I am talking "too much." In new places and with new people, I hold myself back and wait for others to share their stories, perhaps listening to that old *"what will people think?"* tape playing in my mind.

I am also aware of other people shutting down when my stories get too long and monopolize a conversation. I try to nip it in the bud, though this is difficult sometimes because sharing is my way of connecting, finding common ground. I know that is how I built a successful real estate career. I could always find common ground by asking a few questions, then respond to their answers with a story of my own. It seems as if I have a story for everything.

Yes, I've been known to talk too much, but I've also been on the receiving end. When others go on and on, I feel the same frustration I've seen in others; this has helped me practice listening from a quieter place instead of always thinking of the next story to tag onto theirs. I no longer ask so many questions either.

Asking questions is indeed a way to get to know someone; however, when people ask continuous questions it's also a way of avoiding talking about themselves. Therapists are masters at asking questions and are taught not to share themselves personally. A friend who was a therapist used to drive my family crazy with all her questions, but when I asked her why she never shared her stories with me she replied it was because I never asked.

Finding a balance here can be tricky, especially if you come from a family that doesn't like to be asked questions. They will share only what they want you or anyone else to know; the rest they keep under wraps. When you come from a family like this it's hard to have close friends; you find yourself censoring your stories and deleting parts of your life that you haven't been asked or given permission to talk about.

I still feel like I'm being seen as that "Know-It-All" whenever I do the talking, even if I have been asked to talk. Yet at the end of the day, this is simply my perception of things; I haven't actually asked for anyone else's opinion. It is here that another of my deeply buried beliefs surfaces to wreak havoc with my days, my perception of another's expectations or opinions.

I am trying, each time it comes up, to recognize it and thank it for its teaching in my life. Recently I gave it a nickname, WOPT ("What Other People Think?") Even in my seventies, part of me still looks for approval in the eyes of strangers, friends, and family. My mother's voice still whispers in my head, carrying with it the additional message that my behavior and the way I show up in the world is a direct reflection on my parents, my family, and my up-bringing.

I didn't know the power that lay in silence, maybe because I don't remember much of it growing up. I was always watching TV and listening to music, and by my teenage years I was going to bed with records playing on the stereo. Of course, once my own kids came along silence was a rare commodity, and it still is now that I have a retired husband whose hobby is TV.

However, when I do get the opportunity to be in silence, especially in my own home or special places, my entire body relaxes, my mind lets go of the endless chatter, and I can "hear" the voices that speak through wisdom and experience. It is during these moments that I realized how truly exhausting it is to be around one who talks incessantly.

My endless chatter, I now know, is the way I cover up my own insecurities. I would come to understand this years later, when I studied energy and how it is choreographed in our lives, both intentionally and unintentionally. I was working with the energy around me, maneuvering in my world to either be "seen and not heard" or to be heard, even when I didn't think I was being seen.

God bless Bill, the psychologist who gave me permission to have a voice, to speak as me, for me and when necessary, to let others know that what they spoke to or for me in insult or anger was not appropriate without my permission. One of the greatest gifts Bill gave me was this simple sentence: "I don't know if you meant what you said, but here is how I heard it and it hurt." When I can remember to use those words, it totally changes the dynamics of confrontations that arise when others try to silence me.

The other gift I hold dear came in an email message from Taylor Madison with DailyOm. I have this one pasted on my computer as a daily reminder of the power of our words. "SPEAK with PURPOSE not with IMPULSE!" Read that again out loud and feel the power of those words. It only takes a nanosecond to breathe that in before expelling whatever words you are ready to share with the world, and it will make a gigantic difference in how those words, and your voice, are received.

I am learning that there are those who want to hear my stories, and that the truth of my journey may free them to take their own. In speaking my truth, I free myself to live authentically.

I am still working on this difficult lesson – or, as Lynn Andrews would call it, my "good enemy" – that I can't please everyone all the time. The important one to please, to find peace with, is me. It is when I give myself permission to share out loud, respectfully and in turn, that my voice is heard authentically. It is when my mind carries on its own conversation while listening to that of another that my thoughts come out too fast, I interrupt and don't "hear" the person speaking to me.

When I let WOPT take control of my voice, it is stifled, muted and inauthentic, coming from my head and not my heart. It is in the silence of my world that I find me, my voice, and the words I must share with the world.

A Way Off the Shelf:
Receiving Unconditional Light and Love

Take a moment and free yourself, allow yourself to receive…

When I find myself overwhelmed by WOPT, I carve out some time to sit in a quiet, private space and just listen. Whether it is snuggled in the middle of my bed or stretched out on the zero-gravity lounge under my favorite tree, I put on my earphones, turn on some soft music that has no words, and I allow myself to be drawn by that music, into myself. I remember to breathe as I consciously pull my attention into me with each inhale, letting go of any resistance I feel in my mind or body as I exhale. I repeat it as often as necessary to "feel" into the moment and be clear with my purpose.

I set the intent to journey to a space or place within me that needs unconditional love and tenderness, a place of no judgment, where WOPT is never allowed to play or even visit. I breathe deeply and move my consciousness wherever it is drawn. I spend some time there, using my breath as a reminder to stay present and comfortable, keeping my mind and my body at bay so I can "see" and "hear" my own wisdom and truth.

When I "know" I am where I am supposed to be, I open the way for this space to be flooded with soft pink light. I see it flowing in from the Universe through my crown chakra and radiating out into this space within me that needs love, pure Love from that Source of All That Is. I spend as much time here as I need, and when I am ready, when I am full, I close the pathways to Spirit and with a grateful heart allow the waves of music to bring me back into the present moment. I stay in this state of bliss for as long as I can, paying attention to anything I hear, see, or feel, for any messages from within, from my God/Goddess, Creator, from that One Infinite Source. This is a sacred time to bring myself present, let go of all those unquestioned expectations and voice killers, and get down off the shelf.

When I get "back," I may journal a bit, or I may just stay in this happy place as I move through my day.

Chapter Five

TOO AFRAID TO GET
TOO FAR AWAY

Acquiescing power, give it all away,
Makes a good excuse not to live your life today.
Fear your chosen lifestyle only if you play,
Take back your power swiftly, live for you today.

College was the logical and expected next step in my life, or so I believed. My older sister was in college but would graduate years later. I would be the first woman in our family to graduate from college. After high school, most girls either got married or went to work at the telephone company, in a bank, as a nurse, a secretary or became a teacher. I chose teaching.

"What about those computer things people are beginning to talk about?" my mother asked. "Won't they replace teachers some-day?"

I had my answer ready. "I figure if there is going to be an auditorium filled with students watching a teacher on a screen, I could be that teacher. Someone has to make the movie, right?"

Now there's a glimpse of the Vicki who may have been trying to get off the shelf.

When I went away to college, I left behind a wonderful high school romance with a young man I knew in my heart I had outgrown. Kind and compassionate, Phil was every parent's dream for their daughter; for my parents he was like the son they never had. He was also fun, and intriguing, had one blue eye and one brown, and was tall enough to dance with – a big plus in my world. He teased me one Christmas by carrying around a ring box. I think my folks were about to have a heart attack. "Put your hands behind your back," he told me one day. "You can feel what is in the box, you just can't open it until Christmas." It was smooth, hard, rounded on top, and narrow. You can imagine where my mind went.

When Christmas came, he and I went off to the living room by ourselves, sitting on the end of the couch that was our private necking spot. He got up and sat on the coffee table so he was facing me, then took out a beautifully wrapped little box.

"You know we're going to be in trouble, don't you?" I asked.

He just smiled and handed me the box. I carefully unwrapped the paper, opened the white box and took out a black velvet ring box. Looking up at Phil, who was grinning like a Cheshire Cat, I opened it to find a bright, shiny, copper penny. Now he was laughing,

"A penny for your thoughts," he got out between giggles.

"My folks are going to kill you for all this suspense," I answered and gave him a great big kiss. I still have that penny in that ring box in my jewelry box.

I had been accepted at UC Irvine and UC Santa Cruz, which were three, or four-hour drives away, respectively; Foothill JC, a couple of hours away; and Coalinga JC. Mom had encouraged me to apply in-state, to schools near relatives so I would have a safety net. I think the truth was, it was so *she* would have a safety net and a network to keep tabs on me. Also, having gone through the college experience with my own children, I know all too well that instate tuition costs are far lower than attending a school out of your home state.

I too wanted that safety net; I doubted my ability to make friends and to thrive in such a different environment. I settled on Coalinga JC, just seventy miles from home. I had a friend there, Linda, who I had ridden horses with in Clovis. She was older than me and had married a rancher in Coalinga, so at least I would have someone I knew close by, and access to horses to ride. The school also happened to be one of the highest academically ranked junior colleges in the state at that time. It was a bit of an old-fashioned campus (it looked more like a high school), and the town was so small it didn't have a single stop light in 1967. It was lovely though, surrounded by foothills and ranches, oilfields, and oak trees, which I found comforting.

Female students under twenty-one weren't allowed to live off-campus at that time unless it was with family. The dorms were full when I enrolled so my parents rented a studio apartment, converted from a garage, about a month before the start of school. That would establish residency in the town and give me a place to live that was close enough to walk to classes. Then, just a week before the start of school, a space opened up. I would be living in the girls' dorm after all, and therefore subject to rules I wouldn't have had living alone. Dorm doors locked at ten pm, and women were not supposed to wear pants on campus; there were specific mealtimes, and you could not eat in the cafeteria on Thursday nights unless you dressed in your Sunday best. I don't think I ever made a Thursday night dinner.

On move-in day I arrived early, found my room, and learned that my roommate's name was also Linda. I chose the bed under the window and unpacked. I set up my stereo record player and put on the Beach Boys as I waited, a bit anxiously, to meet Linda. The day passed; I ate lunch alone in a near-empty cafeteria and wandered about the campus. It was smaller than the high school I had graduated from and only had about six hundred students. I had graduated in a high school class of eight hundred and sixty, with a total school enrollment that closed in on three thousand.

I went back to my dorm room expecting to find Linda there, but it was still empty. I did a bit more organizing but didn't want to do any "decorating" until my roomie showed up so we could do those things together. That's how I'd seen it done in movies. Shortly before dinnertime, a petite woman with short brown hair stuck her head in the door and announced that she was supposed to be my roommate, but she would be rooming down the hall with a girl-friend from her hometown. So much for a new friend. I would be starting my college time alone, but without the freedom of my own place.

I got a job on campus making milkshakes and sodas, floats, and sundaes for students on breaks from their evening classes. It was a fun job but there was little time for socializing as students rushed in and out between classes or sat across the room at the few little tables that were inside. I was the only one behind the counter, so I was kept jumping between the cash register and the ice cream freezer, washing glasses, and making snacks.

I was still alone on campus. I had met a few students but none I connected with, so I spent most of my free time at the ranch with Linda and the horses. She took me swimming at the Palvedero Country Club's pool and I babysat for her little boy when I could.

Linda would, in a roundabout way, introduce me to my future husband. She told me about Danny, describing him as dark-haired and good-looking. He drove a white Ford pickup and pulled a white Miley horse trailer.

I was sitting out front of the Jolly Kone in Coalinga on one of those dress-up Thursdays when I saw him drive by. We didn't meet then, I later learned he was home on leave from advanced infantry training and would be heading out that next week for Viet Nam.

When I told Linda I had seen him and thought he was indeed handsome, she tried to set up a date for us but found there was no time. I was disappointed for me and scared for him at the same time. Viet Nam was an undeclared action of war and the reason for a lot of civil unrest in our country back then. A few weeks later she got me his address and I started writing to him in-country. Though I hadn't even met him yet, this sure helped me stay on the shelf; while the other girls were out there dating and having fun, I had a "boyfriend" overseas. I had broken up with Phil when I left for college, so writing to Danny filled that empty space of "not having a boyfriend." I fell in love with the idea of love when he started writing back. I was building a fairytale romance in my mind, and heart. We met when he came home, and the rest, as they say, is history.

Fifty-three years later, we're still together – through the hard years and the easy ones, years of tears and years of laughter. Looking back, I can say that I'm kinda glad I was up there on that shelf while he was away, hanging out with letters instead of life. Perhaps that was where fate was playing a part in my shelf life.

I met Danny's parents before I met him. His mother, Margaret, was a cook in the dorm cafeteria, and after he told her we were writing she made it a point to say hi. His dad, an old-fashioned cowboy, rode colts at Charlie Araujo's place just down the street from Linda's. Charlie was an icon in the American Quarter Horse world, a licensed judge and breeder of some of the finest quarter horses at the time. That sweet, white-haired old guy was quite the flirt, he was. I remember him telling me and a girlfriend that just because there was snow on the chimney it didn't mean the fire was out." He knew Danny well and introduced me to his father, Guy.

Several months went by and I was content. I was getting a couple of letters a week and had put a map up on my wall, tracking where Danny was in Viet Nam. In early January 1968, he was wounded and sent to a field hospital at Pleiku Air Base. He was there for about six weeks recovering and had more time to write. He even sent me a picture of himself, along with a pair of brass bracelets, for Valentine's Day.

Eventually, all the running around and keeping up with school and a job caught up with me. That spring I found myself at home with a fever that didn't respond to aspirin, chicken noodle soup, toast, or applesauce. The doctor said it was tonsilitis, but I didn't respond to the antibiotics. More tests revealed that I had mononucleosis, the "kissing disease." I had to laugh. I hadn't done much kissing since breaking up with Phil.

After two weeks I returned to school and heard that Danny's mom was asking about me since she hadn't seen me in the cafeteria. I'll never forget the day in May 1968, when I headed to their house after class. As I knocked on the front door I heard crying, then an agonized voice sob, "Why couldn't it be me?"

Danny's mom answered the door, her eyes swollen and red with tears flowing down her cheeks. They had received a telegram that Danny was wounded during hostile fire and that it resulted in the surgical removal of his right eye. His parents were devastated but held a glimmer of hope that it had all been a terrible mistake. The telegram stated that a *David* L. Dobbs had been wounded. There were calls to the Red Cross and to the army base at Fort Ord, California, but no one seemed to have any answers. Three days later another telegram arrived from his commander, who confirmed that there had indeed been a mistake, but only with regard to the name. Danny had suffered damage to the right eye and facial lacerations with embedded shrapnel. He was to be transported to a hospital in Japan, then eventually back to the States.

Danny and I met for the first time on June 11,1968 in a hospital ward at Fort Ord. It was the day after my nineteenth birthday and my sister drove the three and a half hours with me to the hospital. Danny was having surgery that morning and I wanted to be there when he woke up.

I was there, but he couldn't see me, both his eyes were patched. We visited for a while and I left him a little stuffed turtle that he recoiled from, thinking it was a cat. We all giggled. It was hard to leave that day, wondering what lay ahead for us, or if there was even going to be an "us" at all.

When school was over in Coalinga, I moved back to Fresno, into my first apartment and got a job at a Payless Drug Store in the Camera and Cosmetics department. About ten days after Danny and I met at Fort Ord, I was stacking Adorn Hairspray cans at work when I noticed these two nice-looking guys walk in. They headed my way. I stood up as they approached, straightened my smock, and turned to greet them, to see if I could be of any assistance. The blond one looked at my name tag, then turned to the dark-haired man and said, "That's her."

I turned to see this stranger holding a little plastic magnifying glass to his left eye, his right eye patched. He was giving me the once over.

"Danny?" I questioned, though I already knew the answer. His friend Bob had driven him over from Coalinga.

I clocked out for a short break and the three of us went over to the snack bar area. We chatted for about ten minutes, then they agreed to come back during my dinner break. We had such a good time at dinner, I gave Danny the key to my apartment and said he and Bob should wait there for me and we could talk more. Before they left Fresno that night, Danny handed me a ten-dollar bill for gas to come to Coalinga on my next day off; I would drive him back to Fort Ord to get glasses. During surgery the doctor had removed cataracts and metal fragments from both of his eyes. Now, at just twenty-one, Danny would have to wear the same kind of "coke bottle" glasses my great-grandmother had worn. There was little hope of him ever regaining vision in the right eye, but he would be able to see with his left.

That is how our life together began, with me driving and doing and being everything I thought I should be for Danny. Gone were the dreams of meeting "my cowboy" walking down the airplane's ramp. Gone was the dream of the "us" that I had pictured in my mind as we exchanged letters over the past nine months. They had been replaced by a wounded warrior returning to a country where just being a soldier was frowned upon. There was no welcome home parade; he just sort of snuck back into life with his head down and his own squashed dreams for his life. He had planned to rodeo when he returned; now he was being told he should never ride a horse again.

I often wonder where I would be, who I would be, if life had turned out differently. Instead, I found a place to practice and master my codependency, doing what Danny needed, when he needed it, what he wanted and when, where and how he wanted it. I threw myself up there on that shelf in the name of love. Taking control and taking care of Danny became my focus and purpose, making sure he made it through college and into life as normally as possible. I think back and see where my mom took control and managed our family in much the same way, though she didn't do things for us as much as she saw to it that they got done.

Where would I be today if I had moved to the coast that summer with a girlfriend instead of staying in Fresno and applying to the local university and Cal Poly – the two schools I thought Danny might attend. I also turned down a fabulous summer job as Crafts Director at the YMCA Camp I had attended since I was nine. I was afraid to leave town – what if he found someone else while I was gone? Danny was only driving when he had to and had not yet driven himself to Fresno, let alone another hour up the mountains where the camp was located.

My world now revolved around him – waiting on phone calls, finding him a place to live when he decided to come to Fresno State, and making sure he got everything he needed to go back to college successfully. I had lost all connection to any dreams I'd had for myself, to even any knowing that I *should* be dreaming for me. No one told me it was okay for me to go for it, to make plans, to fail and try again, to take risks. I was committed to Danny, still trying to live into that fairytale I had been telling myself for over a year. It didn't help that Danny kept telling me that "my days were numbered," leaving me to only (joyfully) imagine what that meant, what that could mean? Did he feel the same for me, or was he biding time until he figured his life out? It would be years before I genuinely believed him when he said, "I love you," always wondering if I were just there and he didn't think he would have any other options. I chose to believe he was growing into my fairytale and living there with me, even if he didn't know it yet.

Long story short – which, by the way, is one of Danny's favorite phrases – the love story did live on. Yes, I had found Danny when fear of the unknown kept me close to home, but with him I also found a life I loved. The only thing I really remember wanting as a kid was a horse. My parents couldn't give me one, but they were able to give me riding lessons, which was how I met Linda. Now, with Danny, I had horses in my life and a lifestyle that "fit" the me that loved the outdoors and the animals. With Danny, I rode, I roped; we traveled to rodeos together, gathered cattle with his dad and branded calves with his cousins. Forget being a superstar ballplayer; I was actually living a childhood dream just as dear to me.

A Way Off the Shelf:
Listen to the Whispers on the Wind

The wisdom of Nature speaks through the silence...

Take a walk with Spirit, take a hike in nature, take a jaunt down an empty lane or a stroll around your own backyard. The purpose here is to get out of your normal day-to-day and into the outdoors, even if it is just on your patio.

As you wander, sit, or stand, allow yourself to "feel" into the air, to connect with the Wind, be it brisk and strong or simply a gentle breeze. Set your intention to connect with the Wind Spirits and open the "ears of your heart," not your head. Listen for the whispers on the wind. Let them blow through you uncontested, unfiltered, and unedited. Be open to remembering any messages, signs, colors, or symbols that float your way. Listen intentionally, ask questions if you choose and simply be aware of playing with the energy of the Wind. Recognize it as your ally.

Are the leaves rustling? What do they say?

Is there a bird soaring on an updraft that has caught your attention? What does that mean?

Is the Wind teasing your hair as it tickles your nose? What is the message here?

Be open to all possibility as you play with and listen to the Whispers on the Wind.

Journal your discoveries and any ah-ha moments found in the messages or answers you received from the Wind.

Chapter Six

IN SEARCH OF ME

Who's creating the character that speaks the poems,

Writes the message, paints the plays, creates herself,

The character she sees living in someone else's mirror?

When will she "SEE" it is really her mirror

She's looking in, writing about, playing in, and painting?

he next twenty-five years passed in a blur. Danny and I graduated college, got married, reared our children, and settled into careers. Danny worked for the US Department of Agriculture, and I was a full-time Realtor with a thriving business. We had faced ups and downs like any other family; now, with our children grown and in college, I found myself struggling with an uncomfortable pull that I had no name for.

"Be still, be still and listen," were the first words I heard after driving into the mountains. I had plans to hike up to my special waterfall to contemplate a question my teacher had posed to me: "Who are you?" It was the same question I had been asking myself and had yet to receive an answer. She seemed to think I would find that answer in the mountains.

"Pay attention, watch, listen and dream," she said. "I want you to look around and collect things you feel drawn to. When you 'know' you have what you need, find a comfortable place to sit, create a sacred space for yourself and ask your questions. Be still, be still and listen."

I got to the falls early that day and hiked up to where I could create a sacred circle on the rocks. It was a weekday, and as I laid out my blanket, I hoped I would be the only one there. I settled in the center of the blanket, then, using my backpack for a pillow I lay back on the rocks. Above me, the clouds looked like white and gray cotton puffs floating across the cerulean sky. Shadows danced over the rocks and the pond beneath the falls as the wind played in the trees overhead. Drops of water hit my face and shoulders, but it was not raining. I looked towards the falls and there was a beautiful elder woman in the pond, laughing. Her hair was dripping water down the front of her shirt, her denim skirt was pulled up above her knees, and her bare feet were visible through the crystal, clear water. She splashed me again and threw her head back in laughter.

"You are always too serious when faced with a question you think you don't know the answer for. Chill out, chickadee." She laughed again, then disappeared into an opening under the waterfall formed by two giant boulders tilted towards each other. The water flowed off the mountain and was channeled through the place where the stones had grown together to create the falls. I wondered if I should follow.

My thoughts were interrupted by the sound of twigs breaking and little rocks tumbling down the hill, more splashing in the water. I turned to see a mama bear sitting on the hill across from me with a cub between her legs. The baby bear reared on its hind legs and jumped towards me. I found myself laughing at the cub's antics as it tumbled down the pine-needle-covered slope and plopped head-first into the pond. Looking straight up at me, his eyes glistening with joy, he stood and shook himself off. "Playtime!" he shouted loud and clear. His mother ambled down the hill and swatted him out of the water, then the two strolled up the rocks and disappeared across the top of the boulders.

"Wait," I yelled after them, my voice fading into the sound of the water. "I have an important question that I need to have answered. Who am I?" With no answer from these visitors, I settled back on my blanket and closed my eyes for a few minutes, drifting off in the warmth of the sun.

When I opened my eyes, the light was a softer color. I got up and began taking my shoes and socks off, rolling up my pants legs, so I could walk in the water, feel the cleansing energy of the falls. Crossing the pond, I saw a stick stuck crosswise between the connecting boulders in the opening beyond the fall. "*I can reach it,*" I thought. I wanted it, I wanted to go beyond the water and the stick was calling my attention to that opening. Moving back to my blanket, I grabbed the hat lying beside my backpack but left my glasses there so I wouldn't lose them in the water. I also, on second thought, put my shoes back on as the rocks in the pond were sure to be slippery.

"*Am I being foolish?*" I asked myself as that sneaky voice of doubt whispered in my right ear. Almost immediately I heard a stronger, louder voice call from what seemed like behind the falls.

"Be still, listen and come. Come now!"

Without thinking, as if being pushed by a gentle hand at my back, I moved across the pond. When I reached the falls, I stuck my hand out and was shocked by how cold the water was.

"Now!" the insistent voice called, and I felt myself being pushed a bit harder into the water. Turning around, I got only a glimpse of a red scarf and long white hair before I fell through the water into the cave behind it. I reached for the stick to catch my balance, and it held just long enough for me to get both feet under me. Then it released its hold on the rocks and remained nestled in my hand, heavy and dark with water.

Holding tightly to this precious stick, I turned to go back to the sunshine and warmth when I heard that now-familiar voice whispering once again, "Come, come now. Follow my voice and come."

As I moved through the long, dark, and narrow passageway, I could feel both sides of the rocks brushing my shoulders. It was high enough now for me to walk without stooping, and the passageway widened as I walked on, still clutching the stick for comfort. I passed a wolf curled up on a ledge in the rocks, her ears alert, amber eyes flashing with the reflective light of what looks like a fire farther down the trail. There was a blue and gold butterfly sitting on his blackish gray shoulder. Realizing these may be teachers, I asked them both, "Who am I?" The wolf turned his gaze to the fire and the butterfly flitted off into the darkness along the walls, and the only answer I received was silence. My head was beginning to throb, maybe from the cold, or was it fear creeping into this unknown place?

"Do I go on or go back?" I asked myself.

Seeing the fire more clearly now, I decided to at least go there and get warmed up before heading back through that icy waterfall. The passageway grew wider still, and the small cave where the fire was located seemed familiar. I realized that I had been here before, when I journeyed with a Corsican teacher, Josianne Antoinette, after 9/11. She had led me through a pitch-black tunnel into this cave where I would find a guide, a protector, and a place I could come to feel safe whenever I was overwhelmed by fear.

Now, as I approached the fire, WahSo, this friend and protector I had found, came out from the shadows. He motioned me to sit with him, then he put his arm around my shoulders and drew me close.

"You can't go back yet," he said, "you still have a question to answer."

Once warmed, I was led out the backside of the cave into a forested area where I saw an old cabin, which I also recognized as a place I had been before. It was a place I had come to know as my healing lodge where I could go when I needed to "see" quiet eyes, to divine answers to troubling questions.

WahSo and I walked together on the familiar path strewn with pine needles and pinecones. There were ladyfinger ferns and wild roses all about the area and an old redwood tree next to the cabin, its trunk nearly as big around as the cabin itself. It had been a long while since I was here, and I had forgotten how peaceful it was. As I turned the knob on the familiar red door, a raven flew up and into the cabin with me and WahSo. There, by the window, I saw my old friend – an overstuffed, raggedy comfy chair. Draped over the back was a very old red, gray, black and white woven wool blanket. I crossed the dirt floor and sat down, pulled my feet up under me and covered my lap with the blanket.

There was a movie screen pulled down across the back of the room. As I got comfortable, the light in the cabin faded and the screen lit up. I saw an image of myself appear on the screen, then begin to fade.

"Wait," I called out across the room, "I haven't asked you who am I! What are my gifts?"

Suddenly, a hole opened in the throat of my image on the screen and light began pouring out of it. The image of me continued to fade as light poured out of holes in my foot, behind my left knee, behind my right ear, my belly button, and the right side of my back.

"Stop," I screamed, "I'm losing all my light. Wait, why? What is all this?"

"You are leaking energy," a voice behind me says, "giving your power away."

I turned and Raven was sitting on the shoulder of my friend.

"You are looking for who you are in who you defined your ancestors to be. You carry every one of them with you, in you, part of you, but they are not you, and you do not have to be like them. Vicki is Vicki, that's plain and simple. You are a unique and special individual, the sum of all that you have come from, all that you have done and all that you have been and been through."

Wolf came through the door, his amber eyes gleaming, and ambled up to me. He licked my back and tummy, sealing the hole's leaking energy.

"You no longer need to look for you in the eyes of others. I give you back your sense of wonder and remind you to trust what you see."

Tears sprung to my eyes as I listened to Wolf's message. He licked them away, then laid his head on my shoulder for just an instant, nuzzling the hole behind my ear. I heard him tell me to remember to love me so that I may be loved, then he was gone.

I recognized Little Dove, another friend I had met briefly on the beach beside a lake years ago. She came into the cabin wearing white leather robes with a blue and green turquoise necklace around her neck and silver bangles on her wrists. In her hand was a fan made of hawk feathers with blue and green beads. She walked up to my chair and knelt beside me, gently moving the beautiful fan across my body, down my sides and across my back, head, and shoulders.

Stopping at my heart, she told me, "You are a woman. Remember that! You carry the sacred womb within you always. It doesn't matter how you look in the mirror, it matters how you mirror yourself to the world."

More holes were sealed as I felt a peacefulness settle over me. Little Dove stood and for a moment she held her right hand to her heart, then waved it to me palm-up before leaving the cabin.

I looked over toward the window where Raven and WahSo had been. In their place now stood a golden-colored bear smiling, holding a paw out to me as if offering something or waiting for something to come. An exquisite red-tailed hawk flew in through the open door and landed on his paw. It dropped a tailfeather as it flew across the room, and I watched the feather spiral to the floor at my feet. Flapping his wings to draw my attention back, the hawk made eye contact with me as he shared his message.

"You must speak your truth and let go of your attachments to anyone else's opinion. Some will hear you and others won't. That's okay. The ones who want and need to hear you will; the others don't matter. Soar high and see. You must manifest now what you dream, not just the dreams of others. You create and we appreciate."

I looked up at the screen and saw the image of me whole and complete as it faded into the shadows of the setting sun. It was now time for me to go back. Walking out the door, I turned and blew a kiss into my healing lodge speaking prayers of gratitude for this space and all who had shared their messages with me. I was alone.

I closed the red door behind me and headed back down the trail alone as dusk settled over the path. It was a quick return through the cave and a dash under the waterfall and I was back on my blanket, the damp stick still in my hand. I was aware of the hard rock under my back and a weight over my eyes. I reached up and removed it. Opening my eyes, I see a small lavender-filled pillow had been covering them. The evening light was dancing on the pond as I headed back down the mountain to my car.

"I will remember all of this," I yelled out to the trees and the creek. "I will dance in the rain and not surrender to the storm!"

When the question "Who am I?" circles me and pulls me down in doubt and fear, I remember! I remember the wonderful journey I was gifted at the waterfall. I remember the teachers and my friends, and I remember me.

It was time for me to define who I wanted to be and what I wanted to do with the rest of my life. I needed a clear intention to give voice to my truth without any expectations I might have about what other people thought. Happiness was not going to be a destination anymore; it was going to be the attitude I chose to travel with as I jumped off the shelf and began a new journey into the me I was becoming.

I knew time would help me choose the memories I wanted to hang onto and that I could intentionally let go of the rest, writing out of my story what no longer served me and writing in the life I wanted to live.

Expected, unexpected, wanted, or unwanted, needed or not – change is never easy. And as the anger, grief or frustration, anxiety, anticipation, or joy passes through this change, you will always be faced with a choice: embrace what comes over the horizon or be dragged along and fight it all the way.

I made a conscious decision – an intentional choice from my heart – to begin each new journey knowing it would at some point shift and change. One of my favorite reads is the *People's of...* series by Michael Gear and Kathleen O'Neal Gear. The one thing the elders consistently say in every book is, "The world is changing." It reminds me of the inevitability of change, not only in the world at large, but my world as well.

I had to walk into this new journey from a centered place within me that holds all the answers. I would make a heart-driven choice to explore... where do I go from here? It doesn't happen overnight. It takes time to listen and discern if what you are hearing is coming from your ego-mind (that monkey chatter that seeks to keep you planted in one place, safe from yourself and others) or from your heart and your body-mind, soul-centered and spirit-driven.

Scarlet dreams dive deep with the dolphin twins
High arched leap over crested waves.

Summer dreams of sparkly things found
In a wizard's pocket beneath the crystalline city
In the depths of dolphin's dreaming.

The dream of dreamers dreaming is in the
Knowing that they have A Dream.

A Way Off the Shelf: Create a "Fetish"

You will make three different ones: physical manifestations (creations) that represents who you have been, who you are, and a third for who you are becoming.

Fetishes are found in virtually every culture in some form or another; their names different but their meanings are similar. They are a physical manifestation of an intention, desire, or totem. A fetish is usually a small carving of animals, birds, et cetera, but it can be of any form or made with any material. Regardless of its shape or the material used to make it, a fetish is thought to hold special powers, with its purpose being that of assisting the one who carries it – be that an individual, family, or community. A fetish is considered a helping spirit, guiding one in matters of the mind, body, heart, and soul, even the universe.

It is the "owner's" responsibility to see that these special "beings" are well cared for, kept in a special place or pouch. Many traditions gift their carvings with crushed turquoise often mixed with a bit of cornmeal to keep their fetish "well-fed." You make an item such as a fetish sacred with your intent and your blessing.

You are probably familiar with the small stone carvings found in metaphysical stores, tourist stops through the Southwest, even in garden centers and specialty stores. They are often sold with a small card from the carver telling you the story of its meaning.

You do not have to be a "carver" to create a fetish for yourself. The first one I was tasked by one of my teachers to make was difficult for me to envision. She told me in a phone consultation, "Vicki, I want you to find a place in nature and create two fetishes.

One is for your emotions, and one is for your feelings. When you find the right spot, everything you need will be there for you. We will not speak again until you have done this."

"What do you mean?" I asked but the reply was vague and held no instruction or direction other than a repetition of the above. I spent the next several months asking anybody I could if they would explain the difference between emotions and feelings but received no solid answer.

When the day finally came for me to make that drive to the hills to find "that spot" I took along a roll of sinew, "just in case." It didn't feel like glue was an option. There is a lot more to this story in the search for the right place and then the search for "all I would need" to make them. Suffice it to say, my teacher was right and no, I didn't take a knife or do any carving. For one, I found a stick and dried grasses that swirled around it and bark with woodpecker holes to stand the stick in. The other was created with a stone tied on top of another stone adorned with an acorn cap and wildflowers. It had been nearly a year but finishing them meant I could call my teacher and talk to her again.

On another occasion I was drawn to use air-dried clay to create a fetish for myself. After it dried, I created a tiny necklace of turquoise beads and painted it with the designs and colors I had been gifted in a meditation.

The point is that you can make whatever you want, with whatever you are drawn to use. This is not a particular tradition or cultural exercise. It is all about you making something that represents you in the three aspects listed above. Make this about you *for* you, holding the energy of all the "you's" present for this exercise. Gather your materials, call in your muses, light a candle, and enjoy the journey. It is not about art; it is about you finding you and creating something to hold the memory of each of these aspects of you.

When you have finished, make a special place for them to live out in the open or in a pouch; the decision is yours. Remember to care for them, talk to them, feed them with your words, your joy, your tears, your laughter, and don't forget a wee bit of cornmeal and even some crushed turquoise for good measure.

Most importantly, remember their story, and remember to have FUN!

Chapter Seven

I CAN DO IT ALL

Reading friends' words tears flow quiet, salty,

softly cleansing the heart.

You did it again, you did it for them, takeaway, or a win?

Friends' words touch long-lost hopes hidden between the worlds.

Will I, can I, should I, of course, not, let them, but, but, but,

I can do it all ~ And you can die in the doing.

"Hey lady, let's go for a drive today!"

I turned to look towards the voice but saw no one. Thinking I must be hearing things, I started again to get into the car and head to the office.

"Let's go, let's go, pleeeease…" the voice trailed off.

Again, I looked around and there was no one in sight. While driving, I put on a tape and listened to the story of a woman who was out on her own in the wilderness, learning how to survive without a tribe.

Realizing I had been driving well past the length of time it would take me to get to the office, I turned off the story, pulled over and looked around. I was on the back road up to a place, not far out of town, called Lost Lake. I had missed the turn-off to the office and my car, on auto pilot while I listened to the story, had just kept right on going.

"Pleeease?"

I heard the voice faintly now – it seemed to be coming from the backseat. – and finally gave into the idea of taking some time off. I was out, away from town on a weekday with little traffic, and it was a perfect afternoon to just hang out by the creek, watch the birds, the water, the trees, and maybe even drift a bit with the clouds.

Once at the creek, I took my shoes off and walked out across the sand spit separating it from the grassy, tree-studded hillside. The water flowed slow and steady that day, as we hadn't had much rain and there was little water being let out of the damn above the creek. Raven clucked a hello and after a few loud scoldings, I realize he was talking to me, not *at* me. I found myself mimicking his voice and returning the hellos. It was fun to hear his response and try to match the same tone and sounds. When the raven fell silent, ducks called out a warning to those sleeping across the sand, but I let them know I was only here for me today. The sleeping ducks never even lifted their heads as I passed.

I sat out on the rocks that naturally formed a bit of a gateway onto the path to the water. I had my sacred little carry-all with me and, reaching inside, I took out a candle and lit some sweetgrass. The scent filled the air, instantly transporting me into a state of calm and quiet. I inhaled deeply, letting the smoke carry my mind away from the everyday and into a non-ordinary place of being. I understood then that I was being called here today, that there was a purpose, and decided to simply surrender to this moment and enjoy it.

Leaning back on the higher rocks, I closed my eyes against the sun that had sprung out from the shadows of the overhead trees. Its warmth left me sleepy, and I found I wanted to lay down in the sand and absorb the sun from above and from the warming sand beneath my bare feet. I moved over to a clear spot on the spit and laid down, squishing my bottom and shoulders around under me until the sand formed a pillow-like shape that supported my curves.

I'd been struggling with thoughts of a friend that was always in need of something. She popped into my head and my monkey mind started stirring up every reason she had asked for help, mostly financial, for most of our friendship. Lately, I had been coming up with excuses, very real ones, as to why I couldn't give her money, but I helped her find things she could do to earn the funds she needed. It took me over a year before I could say a definitive no, working up to it in increments of "I can do this much but I don't have that much."

My back started aching, and as I sat up the little voice in my head whispered, *"Backing away from your power again, eh?"*

The sun was now hidden behind darkening clouds, and as a chill ran through me, I wrapped my arms around my shoulders for warmth. Suddenly, I felt *other* arms wrapped around me from behind. I tried to twist around to see who it was, but I was held tightly by the energy holding me.

What is this energy all around me? Around me, I thought, *not next to or with me, but surrounding and crippling me.* That's when the "ah-ha" light popped on; suddenly I could see how my overextending myself in service and assistance to others was a crippling energy. It was the ultimate power-grab, disempowering me from being of service to myself.

"Sometimes, Vicki, one of the most helpful things you can do for another is to let them learn stuff for themselves, at their own pace.

It is also one of the most helpful things you can do for yourself. Empower, celebrate, and free them all."

–The Universe (via Andy Dooley)

Tears began to fall as I saw the imbalance in continual giving, giving, giving, and doing, doing, doing. Not only do I rob the person I am "doing for" of their own experience and the lessons waiting for them, I am draining myself of my own power, giving it all away.

I felt the energy that has surrounded me release its grip, then begin to materialize into the form of a Rubenesque, grandmotherly-type woman, full-figured and round, rosy cheeks, and twinkling eyes. Leaning forward, she whispered in my left ear, "The balance of power comes when you learn to receive as well as give. When you can accept the generosity of others, there will be more generosity attached to your giving and instead of leaking and sucking power, there will be a balanced exchange over time. That balance," she explained further, "also requires that you nurture yourself right along with the rest of the people in your life so that you are equally as important as they are. Go now."

I picked up my things and hurried back to the car in the shadowy light of the setting sun. There was a little journal in my glovebox, and as I jotted down some notes about the message I had just received, an old quote from my church days popped into my head: "It is better to give than to receive." Were these conflicting messages?

76

I had been brought up to do for others. Not realizing how unhealthy my translation of that was, I spent much of my time, energy and money "buying" people into my life in the name of "service." It had become more than a "lifestyle"; it had become an addiction. Now my mind was spinning with how I could help and support people I came to know without disempowering their journeys. What I heard in that next moment was life-changing.

"You teach them to fish and stop continually giving them fish!"

Knowing this and putting it into action felt very foreign to me. I had taken on the mantle of "I can do it all." If someone needed something, I made sure it got done or they got it. I knew it was my job to set the tone in the family (Thank you again, Mom!) and I couldn't let anyone down. I wanted everyone around me to be happy. That made me happy, or so I thought; yet I was not living in a way that filled my home or myself with joy, and I blamed myself for not getting it right.

In retrospect, I don't think my loved ones were happy either. My husband was distant, and how could he not be, with me working, coaching, teaching, doing constantly? My teenage children were now bickering with each other all the time, and while that is not that unusual for teenagers, I knew this went deeper. My daughter was angry and uncommunicative. I tried to be whatever I thought she needed me to be, she just wanted me to leave her alone. My son was the happy-go-lucky one. Like me, he kept himself busy with his "own thing" and out of the energy of conflict. Looking back, I realize he was mirroring me, masking his discontent by staying busy.

I was losing control of my life, my family, and my world and knew I had to do something soon or we would all sink.

Sadness hung in the space around me, like an incoming storm.
I could feel the heaviness in the air and smell the rain.
The storm is palpable, it feels like it will rip through
the middle of everything I love.
Or will it just rip through the middle of me?

I read in DailyOM "that in the most ideal situation, the person we are helping sheds light on our own dilemma." When someone, whether we know them or not, is vulnerable enough to ask us for help, the finest gift we can give them is to meet them without judgment and with that true knowing that we are not "better than" simply because we are in a position at the time to help.

I began to use discernment, to be sure that my tendency to give was not coming from a need to feel good about me but from a place of true service. I took a moment before I jumped in with both feet to feel into the situation so I could be impeccable with my decision. "Giving and receiving are companion energies that take turns throughout our lives," The DailyOM article continued. Indeed, this was a big lesson for me, learning to receive as easily as I had mastered giving.

I remember the first time I was very conscious in my decision to "assist a fisherman" rather than giving them a fish. I had read a GoFundMe request on Facebook, and being in a financially fit place in my life for a change, I made the decision to support their request with a donation. Just before I hit that send button, I felt those all-encompassing arms surround me, holding my arms to my side. That was all it took to remind me that I had other options I could offer that would give this person a chance to "earn" what they were needing. It turned out to be a wonderful opportunity to get to know a relatively new acquaintance and we have been friends ever since. She earned what she needed, taught some beautiful people in the process, and gifted me with her tenacious spirit and wise words. I will forever be grateful for that Facebook post and for Grace, who met me with her own impeccability and with integrity.

A Way Off the Shelf: Intentions and Recap Basket

I discovered a wonderful exercise that has helped me when I had a tough decision to make. It even helps me accept whatever decision I have made, especially those made without thinking or when I felt pressured and was suffering from that old familiar "speech impediment" (I couldn't say no).

There is an old indigenous tradition that makes use of a "Burden Basket," a small basket you hang or place by your front door. When you come home, you place the burdens you have carried that day in the basket so you don't carry them into your home. Conversely, when you leave your home, leave any burdens you are carrying from your home life in the basket so you don't "burden" the world with them.

I devised a different "game" for myself, one that helps me stay aware of the way I have "played" out my day's hand. I keep a small basket on the table in my necessary room with a few tiny crystals and some crushed turquoise. Sometimes I drop a leaf of sage in it or a pinch of tobacco. It turns out this is a good place for a moment of quiet contemplation and reflection, I keep a little stack of small papers and a pen beside the basket.

In the mornings, I take just a few minutes to think about my day and how I want to "be" in that day, and what I want to be doing. I write them down, sometimes in the form of a prayer; sometimes I just draw a symbol that works for me in that moment. Sometimes it is one word, like clarity or charity or fun or communication; other days I am more specific. When I am done, I fold it up tiny and place it in the basket and let go of any expectations or thought up outcomes. Then I'm off with my intent as my companion for the day.

In the evening, during that last visit to the necessary room before bed, I take a few moments to recap my day. I think about what I have done well and what I may have not done so well. I accept responsibility for it all and, on one of those little papers I acknowledge what was good in my day and forgive myself and others for what may not have been. I metaphorically "unload" those thoughts and that energy. I place them in the little basket with my prayers and hit the hay, light and free of all the chatter that used to go on in my head. I fall asleep faster, sleep better, and wake easier when I have done this.

The next morning, before I add to the basket, I take the tiny papers from the day before out of the basket and lay them aside or put them in another container. I will take them outside at some point and bury them, shred them to the wind, dissolve them in the rain – in other words, let them go. Then I write my day's intent and get on with my day, walking out with a clear intention to be the best I can be, to do the best I can do, and to give and receive where I am needed and when I am in need.

Chapter Eight

GRIEF, A HARSH TASKMASTER
AND MASTER TEACHER

Grief is like an ocean wave, gentle at times and deadly at others.

Sometimes I stand on the shore and a little wave comes in and circles my feet and I can feel the sand move out from under me, but I stand strong and firm in my place and the ground hardens again beneath me and I find my balance again.

The next time I stand by the sea the wave coming in looks almost rideable, knee-high, maybe fun to flow with until it hits me knee-high and about knocks me off my feet. I struggle with the pull of the undertow and the power of the wave and helplessness begins to surface. But just as I feel I will topple over; I find my feet under me again and the wave is receding. I wonder what ever made me think that might be fun.

Maybe it would be better if I stayed away from the sea.

Oh, but the draw of the ocean, the rhythm of the tides. The sound of the waves rock me to sleep and to her shores I return. Look! Here comes another little one, a gently rolling softer one moving quietly towards me. These are easy now,

I know I can stand my ground and only be rocked a bit by the current.

Wow! Look out there. That one looks like it is as tall as me. It could carry me to the clouds, and I could fly, couldn't I? And then it hits me chest high and I am knocked head over heels, swallowed by the water and pulled down and down and around and now I can't breathe. Fear circles and terror pushes me further beneath the sea and wait a minute.

Is this a calmness coming over me?

Goodbye fear. I like this place. It is calm and smooth, and I can let go of all the stuff around me and just let the sea carry me... away. And then I am thrown out of the wave and onto the shore and left breathless and exhausted, wondering how I ever made it through that wave. Wondering even more why I even made it through that wave. Wishing I could go back to that place of calm peacefulness but knowing it is not my time. The sea didn't spit me out, I chose to come back. I have to stand back up and face the sea and wait for the next wave to wash over me.

Look here comes a little one. I can handle this one...

Another day, another wave, standing in the sand, waiting, and watching.

Still loving and remembering.

"*D*id you hear that scream?" I asked as I nudged Danny. We were watching a movie in bed and I guess he was asleep. He just mumbled, "It was probably the foxes."

There were two or three that lived under an old fig tree on the abandoned property next to us, the freeway that had taken the house that used to be our neighbors'.

"I don't think so," I said as I got up. He was already back to sleep. I swear, that man can sleep anywhere, anytime. He just closes his eyes and he's out.

I got up to investigate the sound when I heard it again. It sounded like it was coming from behind us, not from the direction of the fox den. The sound was more like a bird's scream, like it was being attacked.

I went out back and sat at the end of the pool, listening in the silence of the night. Nothing. The night air was cool for June; I drew circles in the water and looked up at the stars. In that moment, a "whoosh of wings" sound came from the pine tree next door and a large white bird flew out of the top branches, circling me clockwise at the pool before returning to the tree. Totally surprised, I picked up the flashlight I had brought with me and shined it up through the branches. Out flew the bird again and circled twice more before landing back in the tree. I caught it in my light as it landed, a barn owl or ghost owl, as it has been called, with its big round, flat white face. I went back to bed grateful for the sighting and the call. I had never seen an owl around the property in the twenty-seven years we had lived there. I would wonder about the message from Owl, just as I had that morning some four or five years earlier when a cacophony of birds screeching had awakened me at first light. When I went outside back then, I had found no sign of birds, just feather gifts. This time it would be just a memory until its meaning became crystal clear.

In Ted Andrews' book, *Animal Speak*, he explains the symbolic meanings of the owl: intuition, the ability to see what others do not see. The presence of the owl announces change, the capacity to see beyond deceit and masks, and wisdom. The traditional role of the owl spirit animal is the announcer of death, though it's often symbolic, like a life transition or change. I came to understand weeks later that Owl had been preparing my soul for what was coming in the weeks ahead.

As 2005 got into full swing, I was well into my spiritual journey. I was beginning my fourth year in the mystery school, finding my way back to peace and balance in my life, and putting into practice the tools and techniques I was learning. Danny and I were "dating" and making time for each other.

A year earlier, at an event in Hawaii, Lynn Andrews had gifted me with a powerful message: "If you want to build a new kind of relationship with Danny, you will need to mirror for him who you want him to be for you.

My first thought was, *"Damn, it's all my responsibility again."* Then I realized she was offering me her personal version of 'do unto others as we would have them do unto us.' Mirroring to them meant reflecting to others, the image of who I wanted to "see" in the people I loved and cared about. It meant being authentic, real. It meant being me. This powerful, life-changing practice was now changing my life and my relationships in a positive and wonderful way. It was not an easy lesson to keep up with, but one that was well worth the effort when I remembered.

Danny and I were out-of-debt empty-nesters with both of our children finished with college and married. Life was good. He was retired; gone were the stress and anxiety that he lived with all those working years. I was off the shelf and enjoying life, work, my spiritual community, and falling in love with my husband again.

I was creating and teaching workshops incorporating the information I had learned from several spiritual teachers. Creativity was becoming a huge part of my world. I loved using art and crafts in my workshops. Projects were designed to anchor the teachings into a physical piece or a practical tool for my students to use or to revisit and remember what they had learned or discovered for themselves.

Raney and her husband Scott were going to move back to California from Colorado when Scott finished his Ph.D. studies at CSU Fort Collins that fall. They decided it would help to get her horse back to California ahead of their move and I was up for a road trip myself. It was the latter part of June and a perfect time to cross the country, meandering down whichever road called my name. Armed with maps and Nigel the Navigator (a handheld Garmon GPS), I headed off to Colorado. My dear friends MossRock and Lisa had named Nigel when they borrowed him for a trip they made here in California. I had programed him with an Australian male voice, and we all laughed at his interpretation of some of the Spanish words on our maps. The plan was to visit friends along the way and just dawdle, rather than driving straight through to Colorado.

I stopped for a walkabout break in Nevada, just before the Utah border and made thirty-five dollars on a penny slot machine. When traffic on the I-15 slowed to a crawling stop because of fires ahead, I got out the map and, recognizing Green River as a place we had stayed on previous trips, I took to the shoulder and drove to the closest off ramp. The next morning, looking at the map, I saw I was close to Bryce Canyon and decided on another detour that would take me through Bryce and Canyon of the Arches National Parks. I spent the night with friends and headed north through Boulder on up to Fort Collins where I found Raney loaded up and ready to head out the next morning.

We left early on the morning of June 30th. We were hauling Raney's quarter horse stallion Junior, to our home in Clovis, and to help with travel expenses, a friend's gelding to southern California. Wendy's was our favorite stop along the way. They had a great fruit salad with yogurt dip. I ate the cantaloupe and grapes. Raney ate the honeydew and watermelons.

We had just left a Wendy's in southern Utah when Ryan called. He was worried about his puppy that was at the vet with parvovirus. He had worked later than usual that afternoon and wasn't going to have time to go by the vet to see him before getting to his ranch to take delivery of a load of sand for his round corral.

I told him to call the vet and at least get an update on his condition.

He called back about twenty minutes later. "Mom. Dirk's doing great. Doc said he can come home tomorrow."

He was excited and you could hear it in his voice. We chatted for a few minutes and talked about his plans for the round corral he was building. Abruptly he said, "Hey, Mom. Herb's here with the dirt, I gotta go!"

Ryan was building a round corral so he could start breaking the foals his wife's mares kept having. He would rather rope than start colts, but Ryan was an avid horseman, an exceptional farrier, a handyman deluxe, and he loved her.

About thirty minutes later, my mom called asking if Scott was with us. That was weird, I thought, as she knew Scott had stayed in Colorado, that just Raney and I were driving the horses home.

"I just have a question for him, I'll call him in Colorado," she replied to my query. A few pleasantries were exchanged, and we hung up.

Our itinerary would take us across the corner of Arizona into Nevada, where we had reservations at a horse hotel for the night.

"Did you see that crow, Mom?" Raney asked, "It just flew across the highway."

I was always watching for birds and animals on our trips, down back roads, in the trees and on telephone poles.

"Wonder what its message is for us today?" I answered, always thinking about the meaning and messages that are there for the inquiring mind to discern.

When we pulled over for the inspection station at the Arizona border, I stayed in the truck. Raney went inside with her paperwork to check the horses through to Nevada. A few minutes later the phone rang. It was Ryan's wife.

"Hey Em," I answered.

She mumbled something I couldn't understand, but I could tell she was crying. She was saying something about Ryan but again I couldn't make out what she was saying.

"Slow down, Emily, I can't understand you," I said, panic beginning to rise in my throat as her voice broke hysterically. She must have handed the phone off, because the next voice I heard was her sister, Katy, trying to tell me there had been an accident. My heart now in my throat, I screamed into the phone, "What's wrong, what's happened?"

The next words that I heard would not just change my life, they would stop my world.

"He's dead." she cried, "Ryan's dead. He was electrocuted when the dump truck with the sand hit the powerlines."

"No, no," I heard myself saying out loud. "Please, donate what you can, even if it is just the corneas. He can live on through that gift."

I don't think anyone heard me. I don't remember the rest of the conversation or the hang-up because my brain was bantering on about how it could have happened. *"He must have pulled the lever to dump the sand,"* I thought, *"That's why he died, and the driver didn't."*

At the same time, that incessant voice was yelling, *"Why aren't you screaming? You should be screaming."*

I got out of the truck and walked around, my mind trying to wrap itself around those words: He's dead. I called my husband and learned he already knew. There was just silence between us and then we hung up, the tears beginning to flow.

"Where is Raney, should I go inside? Oh God, how do I tell her?"

And the screams finally come. "No, no, no…"

But even then, as I sat down on the wheel well of the horse trailer and screamed, it felt fake, not real. I got up again and paced the parking lot, alternating between sobs and forced screams.

That's how Raney found me when she came out of the inspection station. In between sobs and my telling her he's gone, we got back in the truck. She told me later that she knew something was going to happen when she saw the crow.

Then the telephone calls started. She called Scott; he knew and had already booked a flight to California. I called my sister and asked her to take Danny up to the ranch to say goodbye, as it was getting late and he didn't drive after dark; then I called Danny back to tell him she would be by to get him.

"Please hug him for me," I pleaded. "Say goodbye for me too."

Raney was so strong. She just took over and told me she would do whatever I needed her to do – drive me on, take me to the Vegas airport, whatever – all while trying to hold herself together.

"I just want to go home," was all I could say, "I need to see him. How is this real?"

Numbness in shock *is* real. There is a dead space inside that opens and swallows everything until it fills that pit in the bottom of your stomach and you just want to wretch.

We opted to keep going and canceled our horse hotel reservations. So many telephone calls. Raney calling friends and getting calls from her husband and other friends. Friends calling me and me calling friends all over the country.

As she drove, Raney had to listen to me tell the story over and over again as people I loved and who cared about us called to express their condolences or to ask what happened. Just weeks later I would realize how hard that was on her as I watched my godmother's son telling the story of her passing time and time again after her life support was disconnected.

I don't see how Raney kept driving, but I knew I couldn't. She was moving forward on sheer survival strength and the instinct to keep me going and keep us safe.

By the time we reached Barstow it was nearly twelve a.m. and we both realized we weren't going to be able to make it home that night. Through Raney's horse show connections, we found a place just outside of Barstow to call but only got an answering machine. I left a message and feel so blessed to this day that at midnight someone listened to that message and returned our call.

It took about an hour to get the horses settled in. You can't just put a stallion in any corral. We had to shuffle several horses that were already there around before we got things arranged safely. Raney and I checked into the closest hotel we could find. We still call it the roach coach in Barstow. She got into bed, and I got in the shower and cried.

When I finally got settled into bed and was drifting off to sleep, I had the most real vision I've ever had in my life. It was in color and 3-D. An exquisite white horse was moving away from me. As he turned, looking back over his left shoulder at me, I saw two hawk feathers hanging in his mane. It was so real I remember reaching up with both arms to put them around his neck. I must've awakened Raney because she called out, "Mom, what are you doing?"

Her voice pulled me out of the dream and back into my bed. I told her the story, never thinking that in her fear she would think I was wanting to leave her. I just wanted to hug him, to hold on.

We were up early the next morning and hit the road for the four-hour drive home. More telephone calls, more tears, more stories, and silence. Oh, how the mind does go nuts in the silence of grief. I think the stories keep the madness at bay, but grief this deep doesn't ever go away.

We drove into our place about noon. Danny was standing out back by the horse corrals with his brother John. We hugged, I cried, he felt distant. All I wanted to do was see my son. I wanted to go to the ranch even though I knew he wasn't there. Danny didn't want to go back so Raney drove me up the hill to Ryan's property. In my heart I knew he was gone but my mind wouldn't let go of the idea that he might not know that. I was scared to death he would still be there in that round corral, wondering what all the commotion was about.

When we got to his ranch, Emily and her mother met me, then we went back into their bedroom where she showed me his briefcase and asked me about some papers. I just wanted to be outside. When I finally got to go out to the round corral, there were several people standing there with Raney. Emily introduced them as an attorney, a private investigator, and the assistant DA, who was a friend of hers and Ryan.

I walked around on the inside of the corral and, thank God, I could not feel him there at all. I don't know what that would have felt like had he been there; I just knew he wasn't. When I walked out the gate, I collapsed onto the ground beside a tree he had planted earlier that year. My hand sinking into the dirt hit something hard and as I pulled it out of the sand. It was his sunglasses. I clutched them to my heart, knowing it was his way of letting me know he was gone, and he was okay. In that same moment, I wondered if I ever would be okay again.

I watched the private investigator put a chain and padlock on the round corral as they talked about the local utility company's liability and an investigation. Raney and I left, me clutching his sunglasses in my hand, and came home to find friends gathering to support us.

"Mom, what are you looking for?" It was late Friday night, the day after he left, and Raney was following me around the house.

"I can't find his blanket," I cried. "His baby blanket, I can't find his red and blue blanket."

Danny didn't have a clue how to help as I went on a mad search through closets and drawers and under beds looking for Ryan's blanket. I needed something of his to hold, to hang onto. I finally succumbed to the exhaustion and fell into bed with just the Garfield pillow my mom had made for him.

Saturday morning came and I hadn't "seen" my son yet. His leaving was still floating between reality and a dream, and I needed to see him to know it was real. What I didn't know was that I had no control over any of the decision-making around what would happen after his death.

I was still waiting on Emily to choose a funeral chapel so his body could be released from the morgue. When the arrangements were finally made, I found out I still couldn't see him without her permission. A parent has no say after their child marries; all decisions are made by their spouse, and she had declared that there would be no funeral, no viewing, no celebration of his life.

Late Saturday afternoon I finally got the call that I could go see him. Three of my girlfriends had come into town to support me; they drove me to the funeral chapel. Danny had already seen him, and Raney did not want to go. Doug, one of Danny and Ryan's dear friends who was more like a big brother or uncle, also came to the chapel. My friends waited outside while I spent some time with Ryan. It was hard to even hug him, the smell of formaldehyde was so strong, filling every breath so I couldn't breathe. His right hand was frozen in just the right shape to hold mine; it also had the only visible mark of any trauma: a small, dried blister in the palm of his right hand. I didn't know how to walk away from him, Doug held me up and we cried together as we left.

I don't remember much of the next several days. Family friends and Ryan's friends gathered in our front yard on Saturday evening for an impromptu barbecue Doug had put together so we could share stories and love for Ryan. It was all very surreal.

LIFE itself is surreal, it's all madness... calm and crazy, real and unreal. Nothing matters, and everything matters.

Nobody got to say goodbye, there was no one else allowed to visit him. You don't think about the power and need of closure until there is none. I wrote an obituary for the local paper and invited everyone to a celebration of his life and memorial roping that would be hosted by one of his best friends a month later. I spent the next several days in a bit of a blur, gathering all of "him" that was still in our house, going through photographs, and sleeping the pain away.

I woke up on Wednesday morning, day six, with this intense, nearly desperate need to see him one more time before he was cremated. I was afraid it was already too late but when I called the funeral home, I was told it wasn't, but I couldn't come down until they checked with Emily as she had left strict instructions that no one was to see him. Late Wednesday afternoon the call came that I could go down for a final goodbye.

I held my breath and with closed eyes, laid my head across his chest. As I hugged his cold, still-hearted body for the last time, my hand began to tap a drumbeat that resonated through his hollow chest. A song formed in my heart and I began humming, then I heard myself singing in my head. Looking up into Ryan's closed eyes, I saw a trickle of blood ooze from the corner of his left nostril. In shock, how could that be? A mother's instinct reached up to wipe his nose, his blood returning to me. I took the scissors I brought with me and cut a lock of his hair and then cut my own. I kissed his cheek as my tears soaked mine. I placed a hawk feather in the pocket of his shirt. He had drawn me to him for a final ceremony. He had called me to him with a final gift.

Ryan had given me a song and a drumbeat to use on those nights when I couldn't sleep. I would tap the mattress with my fingertips, and as it resonated his drumbeat back to me, I would get lost in the song and drift off into the dream.

I left the chapel that day and called my dear friend Patty. She and her husband and son had a drumming group called Spirit Warriors. I told her I needed to hear the drums and I drove home to mine. She called back when their group was together at their drum, and they drummed and sang for me and for Ryan. They sang Amazing Grace in Mohican and drummed their blessings to me, for me, into me, with love from Ryan.

When you experience profound loss in whatever form it comes to you, in that shock and sadness, you may want to just crawl under the covers and stay there, to withdraw from life. I did just that until my daughter said, "Mom, I'm not leaving until you get up, get dressed and feed yourself!" What choice did I have? She had to go back to Colorado and to her own life.

The truly unfortunate part of such a horrific and sudden loss, is the shock that resonates through every aspect of your life and the lives of all those who are touched by the same loss. Our expectations of the way someone should react are often met by devastating disappointment and, eventually, deepening depression or outbursts of extreme anger.

For me, it was both. I energetically lost both my mother and my sister as the lines were drawn and the stakes claimed in what would end up being a probate that would tear my family apart. It felt to me like they cared more about his widow than they did me, as though I didn't hurt for her as well. As for Emily and her family, in their grief and in the control I'm sure they felt they needed to survive this themselves, they shut me out of what could have been a time of coming together in shared stories and mutual compassion. Instead, it turned into a miserable court battle over silly little things as Danny and I were openly accused of trying to take his ranch.

When someone passes in California without a will, probate law gives half of their estate to their parents and half to the spouse. On the morning after Ryan's death, Emily's father sat with my husband under the Ash trees at our house and asked him what our intentions were. I wasn't home yet, so he alone had to endure the questions, the assault and madness of what's mine, ours, his, theirs. *Our intentions?* What did he mean? We had just lost our son!

Where did this all go wrong? When did a family steeped in gospel-fed religion turn into a family determined to bury mine, even as they asked if they could pray for me?

Grief is an awful taskmaster and a master teacher of life lessons, good and bad. Grief mirrors the best in people and unfortunately, the worst. It changes people in ways we never imagine as we are challenged to move through it in the best way that we can.

No one got to say goodbye, and that is where my deepest hurt still lies. When the dust settled, it was as though Ryan had never been here. Danny and I became pariahs in the roping world and the horse community we had been such a big part of. Nowhere felt "safe" from the inquiry, "How is Emily doing?" Even my mother was upset when she heard me answer that, "I didn't know, she hasn't chosen to stay a part of our family."

"How could you say that?" Mom admonished me one afternoon as we were going to lunch.

"What do you want me to say, Mom? She has chosen to stay connected to you and Pam, but not to us at all. And to be asked why we are trying to take the ranch away from her is devastating. You aren't on this side of that story. How else can I answer – 'I don't know, because the attorneys don't want us talking to each other'"?

My world as I had known it was no more and never would be again. The Universe asked me to walk this path with grief for many years. As I mentioned in the beginning, Ryan's death was followed by that of my Godmother Ann (my mother's best friend of sixty-three years); then a dear friend from the mystery school was killed in a single-car accident, followed by my only uncle, my oldest brother-in-law and, finally, my mother. They all left in the two-and-a-half-year span between June 2005 and November 2007.

I became quite familiar with the energies of grief and all the mirrors it holds up for people. Our fractured family mirror was falling out of its frame one piece at a time – another probate decision, another trustee, another it should be mine, his, ours, theirs… it was the never-ending uneasiness that grows out of loss, lack of trust and miserable communication.

My husband withdrew from the relationship we had been rebuilding, leaving me truly alone again until we could find our way back to each other. He had lost his best friend.

The drum became a sacred tool for my own recovery, my very personal walk with this harsh taskmaster and teacher, Grief. For me, drumming became the spiritual made physical by sound and motion. It is how I began communicating in a way that goes beyond the verbal and touches those hurting places deep within. It became my form of prayer, connecting me to God, my Divine source for inspiration and support. Drumming became the gateway I used to find solace and strength, relief from anger and courage in the face of fear; to find my way back to love. The single heartbeat of a drum could bring my body, mind, and spirit together in harmony and balance with a healing vibration that reached my very soul.

When you find a way to bring your pain into the physical so you can feel it, see it, and heal it, you find what I call a sacred tool. The drum became one of the most powerful pieces in my spiritual toolbox, the key to forward movement and healthy communication. It became my gateway back to me and the top rung on the ladder that would help me off the shelf. I had been making drums for several years and now, teaching the art of this sacred creation not only gifted others with a new tool, but gifted me with a reminder each time I shared it, of the essence of the beautiful gift my son had shared with me.

A Way Off the Shelf: Drum Away Stress and/or Sadness

The drums are getting louder, not closer but calling me, louder. I can touch their rhythm. I can feel the pulse of their beat deep inside of me, at my very core, the center of me.

When stress tries to bury me under its heavy blanket, I go to the water.

I settle into a warm tub and sink into the gentle arms of the water, allowing it to cover me with unconditional support. I sink in until it covers my ears, and in that underwater silence I listen to my own heartbeat resonate through the water and back to me. I begin to match the beat of my heart with a tapping of my fingers on my sternum, or breastbone. I listen to the reverberation of my own sacred beat in unison with my heartbeat. This is a lot like the Emotional Freedom Technique (often called EFT or "Tapping"). Developer Gary Craig says, "It can work in a similar way to mindfulness, as it can draw a person's attention to their body and breathing..."

When I take the time to do this exercise, my whole body begins to relax. Humming Ryan's song added to the "drumbeats" creates a magical music that feeds my soul and reconnects me with that essence of me that is stronger than the me that sits on any shelf. This "me" that sings back is the one that jumps from the top shelf in wild abandon and welcomes the day's challenges. It is the wild-spirited, unstoppable me that can take on the world and make music out of the misery that tries to push the ladder away from the bookshelf.

There is a power in the sound of your heart that carries all possibilities... it is the beat of your life, your soul matching the tempo of the Divine. Christine Stephens, MSW, MT-BC of Upbeat Drums shares that, "It is the process of participation that creates change."

Try it sometime and if you don't already recognize your soul's song, this is a great exercise to listen for it to sing to you in harmony with the beat of your heart, your own sacred drum.

Chapter Nine

BREAKING THE BARRIERS

Dreaming dreams forgotten then remembered,
Choking on words left by others
Clogging my throat,
Smothering my soul,
Hidden inside circling the center of me.

No! Not! Never again!
I remember to return,
Galloping into the depths,
Circling the center of me,
I remember!

eginning to feel the pull to something different, I knew deep inside that there had to be a better way. Trying to maintain control in my life was a bit like trying to rein in a runaway horse. The "animal" had a mind of its own and was going to go its own way regardless of how hard I pulled on the reins. There is a thrill in that ride, but at what expense? Will I ride it out, be thrown, end up in another broken heap somewhere, the destination long forgotten?

There is a certain calm that comes over one when you surrender control and just go along for the ride. The difficult part of that release is the unknown destination and the fear for one's safety. Resisting and pulling on the reins to no avail just leads to tension and anxiety coming along for the ride. But when I can remember to loosen my hold, settle softly in the saddle, and gently begin to maneuver the reins in my hands so they transmit firm decisions instead of constant control, the horse will slow and begin to listen, its own fears subsiding with mine. Life is teamwork, me, myself, and I in partnership with an ever-evolving and changing "ride."

I had no boundaries; they were all blurred in the doing and giving to keep everyone else's plates spinning on the tip of their sticks. I was on a runaway ride. It was time for me to stop saying yes to all the things I really didn't want to do and start saying yes to all the things I did want to do.

"You mean it's okay to say no?" that little voice on my left shoulder asked.

"Hell No!" replied that often louder voice in my right ear, "What will people think if you start doing your thing and not taking care of theirs? They come first, you know. You were told long ago that that is the way of the world."

"*Go away,*" I think to myself, or at least I think I am thinking for myself.

Saying yes when I wanted to say no was like hauling back on the reins; it built up more resentment, added to my waistline and put me right back up there on the shelf. Holding back any part of myself kept me glued there. The only way down was to start peeling off all the masks I wore, a different one in every aspect of my life. Unmasking would declare to the world, "Here I am!"

I met a friend, Cherla, for lunch one afternoon. Our friendship had hit a roadblock and we hadn't seen each other in a couple of years. A lot of water under the bridge you could say, for me and for her as well. By that time I had finished the four-year mystery school and learned so much about how I walked in the world. I had learned to recognize different energies, dark and light, and how they affected my life and the lives of those around me. Cherla had been fostering a little boy for the past several years. When he went back to his family, he left a void, not unlike a death, within her. I had lost my son Ryan, and though it certainly was not the same, I felt like we had something in common.

When we met up, one of the first things I said to her was, "I can't be who you think I should be anymore; it doesn't serve either of us. It's disempowering me and unfair to you. I placed my expectations of who you thought I ought to be on you without ever asking your opinion." In trying to explain how I was "growing up," I told her how I had put her on a pedestal when we met. She didn't ask me to; it was just what I did with people I saw as being better educated, better stewards of their finances, better at their jobs and what appeared to be in better control of their lives.

Cherla said that happened to her a lot – she didn't know why – and it created tension in her friendships. I shared how she so openly shared her expertise and was so willing to offer suggestions and help to the people she met. She had a way about her that unwittingly allowed others to step back and let her lead the show, to be the expert (which she almost always was). She was a master negotiator, super thinker and planned everything diligently – qualities I admired and envied. I couldn't see those kinds of qualities in myself, perhaps because I was looking outside of me for validation and approval all while I was giving it away to others. Lynn Andrews teaches that those who upset us the most are our greatest teachers. Cherla had indeed been one of those for me, and I will always be grateful for the years of our friendship.

I have a purpose, or I wouldn't be here on this earth at this time. It is in this moment of awareness that I can jump off the shelf and run head-on into life. I am ready to break through the barriers of circumstance into the arena of all possibility!

This journey is in the movement, not in the perfection of each step, so let's get going! Life rewards decision. Make the decision to get off your shelf and back into your life and do it intentionally.

Each day will stir up its own set of reactions. It is how you choose to react to each life moment that will determine the direction of your life. Intentionally creating life (making those decisions) moment by moment requires that we recognize that we are a product of our past, that we remember the lessons and move forward on our quest. We can give in to our fear and anxiety, wait for others to lead the way and give our power up for grabs, or we can pull on our "big girl panties," as my daughter is so fond of saying, and get in the game. Jump into the unknown, the great mystery with courage, maybe even throw up the reins and ride on, hands held high, laughing joyfully.

The human spirit inside each of us has an enormous capacity to survive every unexpected twist and turn life has to offer. Do you know what kind of life you want to live? I thought I did, but I was in reality, just a passenger in my own life, idly allowing things to happen, situations to change and moments to pass by.

Each of those moments lived and experienced has led me to this very spot here today. I am learning to embrace who I am, to inhale life and exhale regret. Inhale today, exhale yesterday and gratitude.

If I am the sum of all that I have done and been, then each time I find myself on the shelf I have an opportunity to learn from that experience. I don't have to feel guilty about being up there or angry or sad. I get to re-vision those moments as teaching times. Currently, I am writing a new chapter in my life, one in which I am off the shelf and in a moment of intentional living.

I thought I wanted to be successful – to be the best at whatever I did, to be seen, heard, earn the accolades and the trophies; to shine. I was on a treadmill running with the proverbial hamsters in a constant state of movement and doing. I was a self-employed businesswoman, a mother, a wife, chief cook and bottle washer, a volunteer at school and for clubs, a coach, dog-sitter, daughter, sometime sister, and aunt. I stayed so busy "doing" life that I never learned how to be and live life, until one day life slipped away from me and it all came crashing down.

David Kloser reminded me in his book *Stepping Up to the Plate* that "Once I learned I could have control over my thoughts, I could have control over my actions." This might be another way of saying what my own mother used to preach: "It's just mind over matter." When you reach that point where it's too much, or not enough, you think "never again" or "I can't do this anymore," you have just misplaced the key to your toolbox, your own personal arsenal of self-help assistants.

You begin again, that search for something different, maybe better. Where to start? I began looking at my feelings. They are a powerful means to connect me with myself. Look deep and delve into your own deepest desires, your core values and most importantly, your dreams. In my deep dive, I realized that I had never learned how to "just be," to live purposefully, with intention and by design. I wanted to mindfully choose how I lived through each day, where I would exert time and energy and what thoughts would fill my mind. I wanted to choose my thoughts because I came to know that they create my feelings.

There is a Buddhist proverb that says, "There are only two mistakes one can make on the road to truth, not starting and not going all the way." I heard Lori Greiner on *Shark Tank* say to a young entrepreneur, "I always look back to learn. I look forward to succeed."

If your quest is to live an intentional life, to say yes to what you want to do AND to what scares you too, what would be your first, intentional step, your first yes?

Start with your truth! Exhale the fear, inhale your intent, and GO! That's when your life truly begins. There is a sense of freedom that is released when you step into your truth and own it. Own who you are – BE who you are, intentionally. As Les Brown said, "You are never too old to set another goal or dream a new dream!"

"Live your life fully engaged in the passionate pursuit of your dream and have no guilt," I heard Shonda Rhimes tell Oprah. I see that as living intentionally. Transformation can start small. Say yes to playing with your grandchildren. Say yes to just walking around the block or sitting for a moment with a cup of tea and a good book before you fold that last load of laundry. Open your eyes to all the possibilities that lay before you and say a resounding YES. That is the key to getting off the shelf!

A Way Off the Shelf: Food for Thought

A favorite "snack"

IF YOU DON'T ASK, THE UNIVERSE CAN'T SAY YES! You must decide not just what you want, but HOW and WHEN to ask for it! When I made the decision to enroll in Lynn Andrews Center for Sacred Arts and Training, I was drowning in debt. I knew it was not a wise financial decision and I tried to ignore the pull I was feeling. Finally, I said out loud to God/Goddess, Creator, I yelled to the Universe, "If this is what I am supposed to be doing then I am going to need some help getting it done."

The KEY here is that you also must let go of your expectations for the end result or answer and be prepared to respond to and work hard at the opportunities that will come in support of your quest, even when they don't make sense to you. You have to say YES too!

DREAM BIG! Open your life to creativity and playfulness instead of fencing yourself in with lackluster limitations. Don't let your rational mind shut down your dream before it even has a chance to begin to grow. See it, then BELIEVE it. I have found that when I share my plan or goal with someone else, when I give them permission to hold me accountable for my dream, I pay more attention to it myself. A great dream deserves support and encouragement, so don't be afraid to ask for it and be open to it.

KNOW WHAT IS IMPORTANT TO YOU! Identify your core values – not the inherited voices, not the monkey mind chatter, but your true values, the truth of YOU. They are the guiding principles that dictate your behavior, how you perceive right and wrong. These core values represent your highest and most deeply held beliefs and priorities; they are, at the very core, your fundamental driving force moving out in your world.

What lights you up? Are you familiar with the old saying, "If it feels good, do it"? When you are aligned with what your heart desires, with your own authentic truth, doing what you want to do and what fuels your fire, it feels good. That is your truth speaking through your body-mind, letting you know you are in alignment with the truth of YOU.

SPEAK YOUR TRUTH! Make a conscious effort to connect to your truest desires, your own inner voice and spirituality without fear of judgment from yourself or anyone else. Freedom comes to you when you stand in your own authenticity. When I was asked to support a venture a friend was starting, I wanted to say yes, but my whole body was telling me no. My heart was racing, my stomach was alive with butterflies and my head pounded with the desire to do something for and with her, but my heart and common sense were telling me that it was not right for me. I took a deep breath and gently said no without a long-winded explanation that would have had me circling back to the possibility of saying yes. It takes courage to say no, and often more strength than it does to say yes. It helps to know that saying no is okay.

DESIGN YOUR DESTINY! Make your decisions from the point of view of what you want, not what you think you can have. My life has been constricted by what I thought other people thought I could or should do or have. When it comes to making decisions in my own life, I am often derailed by thoughts of "I have enough, I shouldn't want more." These are the voices of my past, my parents and their parents chattering in my head. I know me and I know what I want. I also know it is okay to say yes to myself.

WELCOME RESISTENCE! It's a sign you are on the right path heading towards your higher self. See challenges as opportunities and move forward despite the discomfort. If it didn't matter, you wouldn't be afraid of it not happening. I began to do some traveling when my real estate business took off. I would make arrangements for someone to cover my appointments, book my travel and – wham! – I'd get slammed with business and challenged to leave or stay and work. I finally realized that what I will call REG, the Real Estate God, would throw every challenge my way to see if I could stay true to me and trust that leaving would not mean the end of my business. When I didn't, when I resisted that urge to go and stayed, whatever business had popped up to distract me, would fall apart and disappear. I learned to trust the journey and work right up until I said "see ya" and take off. Resistance is an awesome teacher when you listen for the message and don't shoot the messenger.

GO DO IT! We all possess what we need to be our greatest selves. Are your actions aligned with your values and your goals? Make sure what you do each day is in alignment with what you dream for yourself in the future.

NEVER STOP LEARNING! Education increases your awareness. Seek out teachers, role models and mentors that are aligned with the same vision you hold for your own dream. Thoreau reminds us to "Live our beliefs and we can turn the world around." George Bernard Shaw tells us that "Life isn't about finding yourself. Life is about creating yourself!" You know this, but do you remember?

During the years my real estate mentor, Walter Sanford, held a mastermind event or came into my area for a speaking engagement, my production would increase. I would listen to his talk (honestly, I could have given his talk), and yet each year, each event, I learned something different. Some word, suggestion, technique, or system he talked about would trigger something new for me to add to my business plan. The same holds true for my spiritual journey. Each teacher I sit in circle with, no matter how many times, will share something that will move me, often out of my comfort zone, and on down the path I have chosen to walk. It is never too late to learn, grow and enlighten your life.

As Maya Angelou said, "Courage is the most important of the virtues because without it you can't practice any of the others." Indeed, it takes courage to voice our authentic selves, not what we think we ought to say, but the real truth of our souls.

Have the courage to ask that question, "What lies in the bottom of my heart?" When I put that question to myself, when I looked deep into the flame of my heart's desire, I heard that still, small voice from Spirit whisper softly, "Write, play, create, and teach."

I knew I could teach. I had been teaching in many different ways, for many years. I knew I could play, though I didn't often enough. I knew I could create, I loved making things of all sorts and had been crafting since childhood. But write? That proved to be a much bigger challenge than I ever imagined. I had written ad copy, short articles, workshops, and sermons. The challenge before me, the one whispered in my ear that day, was to write for me. That is a horse of a different color and it took me another ten years to realize that I had been writing for years and just not owning it. I am a writer. I am playful. I am a connoisseur of creativity, and I am a teacher.

PAY ATTENTION TO THE HEART THAT SPEAKS THROUGH LONGING. When you have that feeling of restlessness, that pulling, your heart is looking for a place of belonging. Find small daily braveries, spots of time to remember that this life is holy, that *you* are holy. We become what we pay attention to and the purpose of life is to live and to create… to align ourselves with God, with the Divine Great Spirit, the One Infinite Source, because that is what our Soul is here for. Dr. King would say to you today, my friends, "That in spite of the difficulties and frustrations of the moment, YOU still have a dream!"

Ask, Dream, Know, Speak, Design, Welcome, Go for it, Learn, Be Courageous, and Pay Attention. Now is the time for us to TURN INWARD as much as we SEARCH OUTWARD. It is time to trust yourself, your feelings, and your dream.

Chapter Ten

DROWNING IN DOUBT

A feeling, a hole, the void. Nature abhors a void so fill it!
Stuff it.
Look at the hole, donut hole, yum, stuff it in.
Same hole, different shape filling it and dumping it out.
Anger replaces love replaces anger stuffing tears.
Different hole, smaller, shallower yet,
Still there, I'll share, I don't much like this hole
so I'm gonna stuff it whole.

*I*t was a soft spring day with a gentle breeze blowing through the newly budding trees. Walkingbird, a little girl of about ten, was playing outside with several other children. They were going to play/practice a ceremony today. Birdie was bare-foot and wearing her newest play clothes, a golden leather skirt with a softly worn denim shirt that had been her sister's. This was the year she would be old enough to participate, not just watch. The older girls were beginning to let her join in their circle of play.

One of the older girls, twelve-year-old Sweet Blossom, had

made a broom of cut brush tied with a brown leather thong onto a long stick for the handle. She was sweeping the ground, clearing the place for their practice. Blossom was mimicking what she had seen her mother do, pretending to scatter tobacco and cornmeal where she swept. Another girl, Spring, was carrying water to their "stage." She had formed a small bowl by lining a hollowed piece of driftwood with some pine pitch and wide green leaves from the bushes growing beside the nearby creek. Sky Melody, Walkingbird's older sister was humming a new tune. She was making up a power song for their ceremony. It was to be a song to call Great Spirit to join them along with their ancestors, guides, and guardians as they practiced these grown-up things.

Walkingbird's responsibility would be to hold energy for their ceremony. She sat on her rock, pondering what that would mean if this was a "real" ceremony. She fingered the feather fan lying in her lap. She had brought it with her for this game, their practice. The fan was made long ago from the feathers of her winged friends, Turkey and Golden Eagle, Vulture and Owl. It is made of four "Eagle" feathers representing the directions around their sacred circle. South Eagle, the Turkey feather, represents abundance and nurturing, gifting the tribe with food and feathers, bones, and sinew. West Eagle, a Vulture feather, brings the energy of death and rebirth, of dreaming and of change, the energy of movement into and out of our ordinariness. Golden Eagle's feather is next to Vulture, holding the place of North Eagle, the place of Spirit, inspiration, and awareness. Finally, there is the feather of Night Eagle, the Owl, Walkingbird's dark-time ally that represents the East, the place of the old wise one's presence and wisdom in our sacred circle.

Walkingbird has been given her name because of her connection to, and companionship with, the winged ones always around her. In remembering the story, she began to realize the sacred meaning of this powerful gift, this feather fan. It was given to her by her Grandmother Singing Bird. She loved the feel of the feathers, waving them around, moving the wind about her and those around her.

"Oh no," she thought, "I can't do this, I'm not ready." Suddenly Walkingbird became aware of the huge responsibility that came with such a sacred gift. She felt the pit of her stomach fall to her feet and fill with butterflies flitting every which direction inside, her thoughts jumbled, scattered, and scared.

"How can I possibly be worthy of such a gift?" she heard herself thinking. Her Grandmother Singing Bird was gone now, and she could not run to her as she did when she was little. There were no soft gentle arms to gather her in and comfort her, no one to tell her it would be all right and that she was a good and gracious child, a sacred child, the one that was next in line to be carrier of this ceremonial fan. Walkingbird's mother, who was a midwife, was often gone to other villages and her grandmother had always been the one who was there for her.

Young Birdie panicked when she looked about and saw a group of adults gathering around the perimeter of the ceremonial circle Blossom had been sweeping and blessing. The screaming in her head grew louder.

"I can't do this! I'm not old enough. I'll make a fool of myself in front of the elders gathering and I'll embarrass my family."

"Everyone is going to see how stupid you look trying to act all grown up," a voice behind her chuckled.

Walkingbird turned to see who was teasing her. Nobody was there.

Tears ran down her cheeks. *"Oh, why did I ever think I was ready to play with the older girls, to play at sacred ceremony?"*

Walkingbird dropped the fan behind the rocks, hiding it as she wondered to herself why she had even brought it with her that morning. *"This is just pretending anyway, isn't it? No one will miss me,"* she told herself.

Birdie ran to the edge of the woods, to a quiet place where she knew she could hide and just be by herself, she didn't want anyone to see her eyes leaking. *"Everyone knows I have the fan,"* she thought, the shame billowing in her belly. *"Blossom told Sky who told their other sister Night Song, and Night tells everyone everything."*

Doubt had a stranglehold on Birdie's thoughts and was tearing her confidence right out of her chest. "I can't go back," she cried softly into her hands. *"I'll just pretend I'm sick. I'll get my oldest sister Willow to play my part, she's done this a lot. No one will care or even know the difference. After all, it is just practice."*

She leaned against a giant redwood tree anchored in the rocks beside the creek. *"Silly me, what will everyone think? What do I know about sacred space? How can we pretend to play such a serious game? What if we do something wrong? We might call in the wrong spirits or say the wrong words or move in the wrong manor or, I don't know. Everyone will see us and know we are no good at ceremony, we are still just kids playing at being grown-up."*

Would the voice in her head ever shut up, she wondered as she squeezed her eyes closed, putting both hands over her ears. Exhausted, she sank to the ground as more tears began to make dusty trails down the sides of her face. "Who wants to be a grown-up anyway?" she yelled into the trees, "They don't have any fun. They just work and take care of everybody all the time."

Closing her eyes tighter to halt the tears, Walkingbird curled up in the curve of the old tree's roots. *"I'll just stay here while they play their silly game and then I can go home later when everyone is gone."*

Soft sounds, like humming, drifted in on a breeze, landing on Birdie's ears. *"It must be Sky's humming her power song,"* she hisses, her stubborn streak waking up, *"I don't want to listen… but wait a minute, that isn't Sky Melody, it's the sound of a flute. Who's playing? None of my friends know how."*

Now getting frustrated with the constant conversation in her head and the strange noises invading her nap, Birdie opened her eyes and looked back at the clearing where Sweet Blossom had been sweeping. There, she saw a fire with tall crackling flames reaching into the evening sky.

"What happened to the day?" she whispered "Who are all those people? Where are my friends?"

Walkingbird rolled over on her stomach and peered out from behind the tree. There were dancers circling the fire. One was dressed like an Eagle with long wings for arms and a white-plumed headdress with a big yellow beak. Another was covered all over with black feathers; it was Vulture dancer, with outstretched wings dipping and soaring in the darkening light, its red headpiece reflecting the blazing fire. The flattened face of the Ghost Owl popped out from the dark side of the fire's shadow, circling, swooping and soaring in its dance around the circle. The Turkey dancer, who wore a crown of bronzed tail feathers encircling its head, waved barred wing tips in each hand.

"What is this place," Walkingbird wondered, *"Where am I?"*

119

She ducked back down behind the rocks only to feel herself lifted off the ground and carried by her two arms, struggling, towards the fire, a silent scream caught between her shock and surprise. She was escorted to a large, flat rock along the outer edge of the circle, her "captors" motioning for her to sit. She tried to see who they were, but the firelight blinded her as they stepped back into the darkness behind her.

She sat, terrified, starring at the fire and watching the agile movement of the dancers. A woman sat down beside her, and when Walkingbird turned to look, she was astonished to see that it was her Grandmother Singing Bird.

"How could it be?" she asked, thinking out loud. *"Are you real? Am I dreaming?"*

Grandmother smiled. "Are you real yourself?" She put her arm around Walkingbird and held her calmly. "You have come in search of me, Little One. Why do you think so little of me and my gift that you would toss it away, run off and hide from your tribe, your family and friends?"

"I can't be the holder of any sacred space, Grandmother. No one has ever shown me how. I might screw it up and everyone would see and what would they think then? They would laugh at you for trusting me with such a sacred thing. I have just been playing with it like it was a toy, just a fan. I had no idea how important it was. Everyone will know how foolish I am." Birdie sobbed into her grandmother's chest.

Singing Bird sat up a bit straighter and asked her Little One how she had been playing with the fan. Walkingbird tells her about fanning the air, making the fire in her lodge grow bigger and its

120

embers glow brighter. She tells of cooling her face on a hot afternoon or chasing flies from the corners of the babies' eyes when they were sleeping. Birdie tells her about watching the smoke from the evening fire move in different directions as she made the fan dance with the currents of the wind she was creating with the movement of the feathers.

"I like to feel the air move over and around the feathers. It tickles my cheeks and cools my arms," she told Singing Bird.

Grandmother smiled. "You have been practicing all this time and didn't even know it. You have been playing with your sister the Wind, moving, and pushing her, merging with her energy. You have been caring for the sacred space around you, clearing it with the swoop of your feathers. Why do you think you aren't good enough for my fan? You have taken good care of her, respected her and most important of all, you have used her. She has become yours and you know how to use her well. I have been watching you. Keep doing what your heart tells you to do. Listen to the fan. She will tell you how and when to do what needs to be done. All you need to do is to trust her and lovingly respect and care for her. No more throwing her into the rocks. Wrap her in a sacred cloth when you are not playing with her and keep her in a special place in your lodge."

Walkingbird felt hands on her shoulders, shaking her, rocking her back and forth. She opened her eyes and, blinking rapidly against the light, found Sky Melody bending over her, telling her to come on. They were ready to begin their ceremony. "We need you; it is time for you to come and hold the energy for our ceremony."

Birdie looked down and there on the ground in front of her lay her feather fan. It was waiting for Walkingbird to pick it up and go with Sky Melody to join her friends in their sacred circle. She was worthy of this honor. Birdie looked for the rock her grandmother had been sitting on but it is gone; only a few dark ashes remained in an open space between several rocks, a single raven feather laying in the center of the circle of ashes. The girls scampered off to practice their sacred ceremonies.

Writing this evening, I realized the story has brought up my own discomfort. *"I don't feel good,"* I thought to myself. *"Here come the waves of nausea and the headache. Why now, why again?"* I answered myself silently. *"My body is such a great distractor or perhaps, it is protecting me from the hard stuff, the scary stuff, the out of my comfort zone stuff? I want to go back to bed but that isn't realistic. Maybe a few crackers will ease this feeling, these thoughts about all this stuff."*

Stuff, right? Not as in the turkey stuffing, but in stuffing the turkey, aka me.

I have mastered this one – stuffing myself with food to stuff down the feelings I don't want to feel while sitting in my comfy chair late at night. The TV and food now keep me company in the darkness, snuggled in the chair with my puppy, my cookies (chocolate cake works quite well too!) and my doubts.

My heart ached as though longing for a lost lover without my conscious knowing what the ache was all about. I felt heavy, laden down and held by invisible arms in a comfy chair that tilted to one side. Even my chair was out of balance. Scene right, Vicki on the Shelf again.

Dare I look closer at how I got there this time? As the ancestors keep reminding me, "Sweetie, the world is changing, and you have to design every new day like it is your last one. What can you find to stir into that pot of yours today?"

Then my all-to-familiar companion Loudmouth Lenny pops in. *"You've got vittles to make and shadows to feed if you're gonna stay in that chair. I'm hungry again myself."* I've named that chattery, discombobulating, blathering idiot that seems to live in my ringing ears.

"Wise up, my friend," a softer voice pushes through the other's jabbering. *"Ah, you can hear me today,"* it continues. *"Change your thoughts, change your life! Remember?"*

I was making decisions based on what I thought they (anybody and everybody) thought I ought to be doing. Now there's an eye-opener! I was feeding an energy shadow I had never talked to or questioned, and it was always hungry... *they might not like it... they think I'm... what would they do... wouldn't it be better if...* and on and on and on. So many loud, empty thought mouths to feed without me ever asking them why.

"Why don't you like it/me/that?" I could ask. *"Why do you think I'm...? How would you do that or this or...? What would be better if...? If what? If I did that or this or something else...?"*

"What would it change?" that softer little voice questions. *"Who would get hurt? What are you afraid of? What's stalking you?"*

"I don't know!" screams the voice between my ears, *"I don't even know if I want to know."*

I quote Madisyn Taylor from DailyOm here: "This kind of awareness can be a formidable agent of transformation."

And that shelving voice in my head whispers at a devilish octave, *"I hate change."*

Here I am, sitting up on this shelf, eating and judging my own life based on the voices of others in my head, their voices, their rules for living, their advice, or criticisms. I hadn't asked a single one of them for clarification, for reasoning, for explanations or whys. "Doubt" led the way and I just followed.

I gave the people in my life the power to make my decisions, unconsciously putting them on a pedestal because maybe they had more education than me, more money or notoriety, appeared more accomplished than me. At least, that is how I was seeing them and thought that made them smarter, better, someone to aspire to be without really knowing anything about the truth they carried themselves and what they believed. I wrote their stories in my head to justify acting like and doing what I thought they thought I should be, doubting my own self-worth the entire journey.

I didn't believe in me. It was that simple; it IS that simple. Somewhere I had missed the life lesson that says I have the right to control my own destiny, open my own doors and walk my own path! In fact, it is my responsibility to do just that and not lay it off on others.

In truth, when I kept climbing up on that shelf of doing life instead of living and being, I didn't have any defined sense of who I was, just a real clear picture of what I did, defined by what I had accomplished – the trophies, accolades and awards received. These are vastly different aspects of this human being called Vicki.

I was judging the success of my life based on the success of my children, my career, my relationships, my community involvement, and my doing-ness, even as my waistline grew, stuffed by indecision and unworthiness. Ever wait to the last minute to get your clothes ready for a special event only to find that nothing fits, so you make a last-minute dash to the closest Rubenesque-sized ladies' store for the "right" outfit?

It feels like a giant monkey sitting on my shoulder, laughing, and goading and whispering, "You'll look great in that one in about twenty less pounds; better go up a size so it won't be too tight around the roles." It was his lunchtime, and he was having a buffet that day.

Cherla, the friend I mentioned earlier, was an accomplished, well-educated woman who had taken an interest in me. She was clear in who she thought I should be, and I let her be the "Director" in my life's show. I put her right up there on the "she's got all the answers" pedestal. She didn't ask me to, but I did. I gave her the power to direct my life. Sometimes the pressure to be the person it felt like she wanted me to be was harder than being without her friendship. "I'm a hard friend to have," she'd warned me early on in our relationship. I just took that as a challenge. I could be her friend, just watch me!

I had watched her walk away from other relationships and assumed (never asked) that they didn't live up to her expectations. I set myself right back up there on that shelf living in fear of losing her friendship. At that point in my life, I was an empty-nester living with a husband who was angry most of the time. His work was a challenge; he was nearing retirement, just trying to get to the end of that thirty years and hating every day of it.

I was trying to figure out how to live the rest of my life. Cherla became a beacon, a companion, and a resource for a new, better way of being in the world. And, as she boarded her horse at our place, she got to know Danny, becoming his sounding board for things he hadn't shared since Viet Nam. She was like his therapist/friend: she valued Danny for his equine expertise, and in exchange, the counselor in her listened to his deepest fears.

She loaned me an old paperback, *Medicine Woman* by Lynn Andrews, the pages faded and falling out of their binding. It was a life-changing read. At the time, I thought it was a great story and went in search of all the rest of Lynn's books. I was an avid reader and loved this genre. I had no idea what great teachings those stories held.

Over the next couple of years, Cherla and I shared metaphysical interests. She introduced me to a new world of "seeing" with different eyes. I will forever be grateful for her caring and sharing. I was reading another of Lynn's books, *Windhorse Woman,* while riding a train home from a trip to Colorado. In the story, Lynn is in Nepal. She and Agnes (one of her teachers) are climbing a hill to meet with a Nepalese "healer." Lynn was struggling to get up the hill but anxiously climbing in anticipation of a healing. She was sure this woman, at the top of the hill, had the answers, the way.

When she arrived, this "healer" instantly saw an opportunity and told Lynn that she was tired, that there was a darkness in her and that she, the healer, could help her with that. Lynn would just need to come back that evening to do the ceremony, and if I remember the story correctly, bring a chicken.

Agnes, Lynn's teacher, and companion on the trip, was furious and pulled Lynn out of the tent and shoved her back down the path and down the mountain. "Can't you see what that woman is doing to you?" she screamed at Lynn. "You are giving away your power, your will, wanting her to "fix" you, your life. Not going to happen; she will "kill" you and you won't even know it. You are feeding her with your energy, no wonder you are tired."

This story was one of those ah-ha moments for me. I had given all my power to my friend to "heal/fix" me and it wasn't fair to her.

She hadn't overtly asked for it. She was upset with me for going to Colorado to help my daughter after a car accident. We had talked about it and it was Cherla's opinion that it was something Raney should do herself, call her friends and take care of things. That went against my "mama bear" instincts, and when Cherla left for a business trip to Washington I got on a plane and flew to Montana to be with Raney as she drove back to Colorado. When Cherla found out, it was clear she didn't approve. She wasn't returning my phone calls.

The day I got home from my Colorado trip, I called her again and was surprised when she answered.

"Are you up?" I asked.

"Yes," she answered hesitantly.

"Good," I said, "Open the door, I'm coming over." I hung up before Cherla could say no, got in the car and headed over to her house.

She greeted me in the front yard, still in her pajamas. She was not going to let me in the house. I went up to her quickly, gave her a big hug, stepped back, looked into her eyes and told her, "I'm sorry," I started. "I gave you power over my life you never really asked for. I'm taking it back."

Astonished, she stepped back.

"It wasn't fair and I'm sorry," I continued, turned, and left, vowing to myself never again to give anyone that kind of power over me. In retrospect, I am so incredibly grateful for the lessons I learned through our friendship. Cherla will always be one of my greatest teachers.

I know that was a huge turning point. It was one gigantic leap off the shelf and into an abyss. I had no clue what life would look like without someone else either telling me how to live it or me trying to live it by someone else's standard or perceived belief in who I should be or what I should be doing. Doubt would challenge my resolve every step of the way until I could hold my fist up to Doubt and send it away.

I went home that morning and got out my big drum, my Grandmother Drum, and began to drum the knots out of my stomach. I felt like I had been run over by a steamroller and all that squished-out steam was oozing away as the vibrations broke up the knots.

I don't remember ever taking that kind of stand for myself before. The stakes were high; I was either going to crawl back inside myself and settle uncomfortably up on the shelf or... I was going to drum this tension, these knots, that bookshelf right out of me.

After a while, I laid down one of the mallets and pulled my journal and a pen closer; then, writing with my right hand and continuing to drum with my left, I allowed the drum's vibrations to break up all that pent-up fear and anxiety I was carrying around with me. The drum opened a new channel of communication with my Divine Source, one I could come to for information, inspiration, solace, and solitude. The drum speaks in unconditional love and reminds me that I am worthy of all that I am and all that I have in my world. This Grandmother reminds me that in gratitude, all things are possible, I just have to drum them up and live them for myself in service to myself and all that I love.

A Way Off the Shelf: Journey with Doubt

"Your weirdness will make you strong. Your dark side will keep you whole. Your vulnerability will connect you to the rest of our suffering world. Your creativity will set you free. There's nothing wrong with you."

–Rob Brezsny

When you walk with Doubt as your steady companion, chaos will be a constant tag-along for the rest of your life. Learning to listen to and trust the voice of Your Truth over the loud cacophony of that "other" voice, the one that makes you doubt everything, becomes one of your most important lessons. Taking Doubt with you just makes for an arduous and bumpy ride. Lynn Andrews shared in her writing school that "Doubt will drive you crazy! It is the ultimate Heyoka teacher going forward but backwards. It wants you to hurry up to slow down, fly but crawl, see but be blind … it's okay, but it's not. By using opposites, Doubt jumps right into the middle of your story and you begin to question your truth… or is it a lie? You move from love to fear as you struggle to discern the voice of Your Truth from the voice of Doubt." Wrestling with doubt is a daily experience for most of us.

Have your journal and pen handy as you begin this journey…

Imagine yourself at the gateway of a simple but beautiful labyrinth. You will be carrying a small, smooth gray stone about the size of your palm. It has the word DOUBT carved into it in bold, black letters.

The labyrinth has been created in one continuous inward circle

129

doubling back on itself, the pathway marked by small stones lined up next to each other, showing you the way. Close your eyes for a few moments and "see" this labyrinth laid out before you. It is about twelve feet in diameter, not big by most standards, but perfect for your walk with Doubt.

Pick up your stone and begin your journey around this beautiful circle. It is especially important that you remember to listen with your heart and not your head. Pay close attention to the voices you hear and which "ear" you are hearing them through, heart or head.

As you complete the circular walk clockwise around the circumference, the path turns back and takes you counterclockwise back around the circle but closer to the center. Are you listening? What expectations are you carrying with you? Listen for the voices of yeah (your truth) and nope, not this time (your doubt). Take note of them both. Get to know the voices you are listening to. Begin to recognize the difference between them and how their words are coming to you, through your heart or your head.

As you reach the end of this circle near the entrance and the path turns back once again, you head in a clockwise walk around the circle, moving closer to the center. What stories are playing with you as you walk? Are you rewinding old ones or is there a new story taking shape? Is your Doubt stone getting heavier as you walk, or lighter?

Continue to walk this circular journey paying even closer attention to the voices you hear. Can you tell the difference between them now? Are you beginning to recognize the voice of Your Truth? Is your doubt stone getting heavier or is it lighter? Listen... and walk.

When you reach the center of the labyrinth, there is a stone bench waiting and you take a seat. You lean over to set your doubt stone down in front of you and see two piles of small stones, one on either side of the bench where you are sitting. Looking closer at the one on your left, you see the stones all have words carved in white on them – words like accept, inspire, fabulous, calm, believe, happy, light, in harmony, creative, faith, empowered, hope, dream, and becoming. All power-full and encouraging words. You smile as you lay each stone you read back down in the pile.

Turning to look at the other pile, you notice that all the words are colored black like the letters on your doubt stone, words like anger, frustration, fear, depression, anxiety, sadness, grief, overwhelm, stress, fatigue, unworthy, incapable, unwilling and loneliness. Yikes, you start dropping rocks like they were hot potatoes. Scary almost, how heavy those words make you feel.

Are you listening to the voices that have traveled with you to the center? What are they saying to you now? Are they both talking, chattering over each other clambering for your attention? Can you tell the difference – which voice is loudest?

Take a few minutes and write what you are hearing; write the stories that walked in with you and make notes about the ones that perhaps you dismissed. Write about this walk you made with Doubt.

Are you ready to leave Doubt on the dark pile? Would you like to take a light-filled stone with you? If you answered yes to yourself, yeah! Lean to your left, close your eyes, and allow your left hand to drift lightly over the pile of positive words until you feel your palm begin to warm up. When you do, pick up the stone under your hand and take it as yours. It is your right to be (*fill in the blank*). What stone called you, reached out and asked to walk out of this labyrinth with you? What will you carry out with you to replace Doubt?

It is time for you to journey back out into your world. Lay your Doubt stone on the pile where it belongs and take the "light" stone you chose with you. Retrace your steps out of the labyrinth, back to yourself without doubt.

Remember to record this experience, write this journey and all you discovered about your own doubt, the voice that comes through to you and the difference between Doubt and the voice of Your Truth!

Lynn teaches us, "Anything that is uplifting and enlightening is the truth and anything that is fearful or doubtful is not." Have fun with this experience and maybe write this journey as a poem.

Chapter Eleven

LIFE UNBALANCED, EXPLODES

Love Comes Softly

The flames of love can blind us, bind us eternally.

Scorch and burn and try us constantly.

Like the heat of fire burn through us painfully.

But sometimes the sound of love sings quietly,

Sneaks into us unconsciously.

Settles around us peacefully.

Sometimes love just comes softly.

I had lived with an angry mother. She rarely expressed her anger, but as I look back to write about this journey, I recognize how her anger could fill the room before she ever physically walked into it. She wore an interesting "everything's okay" mask. I think I was eight or nine before I heard my parents argue for the first time. I woke up in the night, heard them arguing, and started crying. Mom came into the bedroom and whispered, "Hush, it's alright. Go back to sleep."

I was sure they were getting a divorce. I wonder if this energy or fear is one of the catalysts of my need to please, to be sure the people around me were happy?

I didn't have a role model for expressing anger or any of the other emotions we all have. I didn't have a mirror for good and healthy communication. I got busy at staying busy even as a kid – Brownie Scouts, babysitting, building forts in the backyard, climbing trees. Life could just roll right along with me. As a teenager, summer jobs and dating took busy to another level and weekends could be filled with yardwork, car-washing, working, dating, or sleeping. Sleep was a great distractor, no worries about being busy or bored, just sleep the time away.

The faster I could keep time, life, rolling along, the less likely I was to confront my own or someone else's disappointment. Nothing is harder on a little codependent's soul than a look of disappointment that can pierce the heart.

I got good at being really good, at whatever I was doing. I had no clue that there was an aspect of living called "being." I was, after all being everything I thought I was supposed to be, right? I would not learn this concept of "being" 'til my fifties, stillness of spirit and mind was not part of our family curriculum. Quiet was, read a book, play quietly in your room. Silence/stillness is a very different energy.

Someone (I wish I could remember who it was and when) once said to me that if I couldn't control my emotional state, I must be addicted to it. Drama, confrontation, anger, frustration – all these emotions bounced around in my life like a big red rubber ball, knocking me about. I had no training in how to deal with or handle them.

Where I was in those days, with my young relationship, young family, and new business, I didn't feel good anymore. I was on the outside looking in at myself sitting up there on the top shelf this time, higher than it used to be. *"Dang, that's a big leap from up here,"* I heard that now too-familiar voice whisper in my ear. *"Why don't we just get comfortable here and leave all that other stuff down there to wreak havoc in your world. It's safer here, no confrontation, no change to deal with."*

Depression is a sneaky bedfellow. It can pull you into its shadow under the guise of ease and comfort, leaving you dangling like a participle at the end of a sentence. *"It's far easier to do nothing than to make change, create waves or heaven forbid, do something for you."* There's that voice again…

Winston Churchill said that success was the ability to go from failure to failure without losing your enthusiasm. I was ready for some new excitement, something to be enthused about, something to feed my soul's journey; to ignite my soul's fire, my heart's desire. Sounds easy, but I didn't know what my heart's desire was.

I remember I was going to teach but felt totally unqualified in my student teaching days. I had no patience for elementary-age children or the high-schoolers, who were so different from how my peers and I had been just five years earlier. They no longer showed respect for their teachers or their school. I quit graduate school and went to work for a veterinarian while building my show dog kennel and making a home with Danny. I remember deciding to go to law school. My gift of gab would have been well served on a silver platter in a courtroom. About the time I was to take the LSATs, I found out I was pregnant with our first child. Law school wasn't going to happen with a newborn and a hubby that didn't change diapers.

From there, my world consisted of husband, kids, home, classrooms, afterschool programs, horses, dogs, cattle and crazy. Real estate came into the picture when one of my dog show buddies asked me to go to real estate school with her. She was successful and hated it. I wasn't successful and hated it as I closed the kennel and continued to groom dogs for someone else, all while trying to figure out the real estate game and continue to take care of all the things that were coming into our lives as the kids got older.

I realized that I had never learned to dream, to see myself as something greater than what I did. I was passionate about what I did, whatever it was, but not in love with it. I was a good coach, an awesome scorekeeper and chief cheerleader and team mom. I did love doing things with and for the kids, seeing them succeeding at their chosen hobbies. I loved photography and bought a good camera for myself for my fortieth birthday (thank you Mom and Dad for the help). I took dog show photos, kid pictures, baseball and softball photos and got good at rodeo photography but I never took the time to really learn about the craft. What I did and who I was all came about as a result of my reacting to life. I had never devised an intentional path towards a specific life destiny. I needed a dream!

I knew I wanted to help others tap into themselves, to free themselves of the dependence of others or their dependence on doing for others. If this were to be my destiny then I would need to learn to ask for what I need and to take care of me, for me.

I would need to stop using external influences and benchmarks as the guideposts I followed. Alison Ellison said it so well in *More Soul, Please:* "I created a roadmap for my value and sense of self-worth based on external messages I learned from others."

That isn't my path, that is a roadmap created by my perception, my thoughts about what others wanted, needed, or thought I should do or be. I would need to find new guides for this journey.

I had been bottled up and fenced in with Fear and Doubt as my constant companions. It was time for me to break out of the illusion of their boundaries and walk on, walk strong, walk with myself for myself, into the next chapter of my life. Worrying about what other people thought or who I might upset or if I was doing something right or saying or not saying the proper things had kept me on that shelf.

Joining a school that taught me about personal empowerment, boundaries, inherited beliefs and conquering childhood trauma and abuse was the beginning of finding my dream. It was the first time, as an adult, that I gave myself permission to do something that was just about me and for me.

An authentic vision of myself began to crack through the masks I wore. Layers of others' expectations were heaped on it from creating external goals, desires, and expectations. Getting off the shelf is going to require peeling back some more layers of the many masks I wore, exposing a "me" perhaps even I wouldn't recognize.

"It will be worth it," I would tell myself and walk away from the donuts. One teacher would tell me it was time to pick up the mantle of my own power and stop carrying others around for them.

I rebelled against the word "abuse." I had no concept of that being an issue in my life. I would learn that this word didn't just mean physical or emotional abuse, it encompassed all the ways our parents and their parents were reared. When you study you, really look back or into you/your family dynamics, you begin to see more than the parent, you begin to see the person that is/was your parent.

There is a form of abuse that comes down through the generations of all parenting. It can be subliminal, completely unintentional, and even unknowingly dispersed. We learn what we live, and in the best of circumstances we live what we learn and pass those lessons, the good and the bad, on to our children. It takes a lifetime to outgrow what our parents do, to and for us, through thoughts, words, deeds, and actions.

I look back at my first fifty years and know that all the guilt I harbored over not getting it right, allowing anger to live in our household, trying to balance the scales between girls and boys, brother and sister, friends and family, was just me being exceptionally hard on me, expecting myself to be responsible for everyone else's life. What I know now is that most of that was not my job. That life fed my frustration, fueled my depression, and allowed unreleased anger to billow into rolls around my middle.

Usher says, "Don't step with anger, step with clarity!"

This one really touched me deeply. Not only had I stuffed my life down my own throat, but I was really pissed off at it. I could feel all those years of tanked emotions, all the yeses that should have been noes filling my belly, the void that food filled when the nights got quiet and the refrigerator was my only friend.

As an adult, I married an angry man, a Vietnam vet who received no help and even less support from the world when he returned. Not only was he physically wounded, but as we have come to learn and publicly acknowledge in our world today, he would suffer the effects of PTSD which, when expressed as anger, is terrifying and contagious. His journey became mine before I ever learned that I could and should dream and manifest one that we could be partners in.

Anger was Danny's go-to emotion whenever anything changed, challenged, or threw him off-center. Even his night dreams were angry. I learned anger and the power it held to capture and control. I even mastered getting angry first to engage the explosions before they exploded all over me. He was comfortable with anger and familiar with it; it became his way of communicating his feelings.

My mother counseled that it was the woman's place to set the tone in a family. It must have been my inability to hold that vision of perfection that she carried that let things get out of hand when anger showed up.

I didn't know anything about PTSD; the world hadn't labeled it as a dis-ease yet. I didn't know anger was contagious. I didn't even know what I didn't know, but I learned anger well. It is one of the fastest ways I know to blow myself right back up there on that good ol' comfortable shelf, because after the explosion, there is a calm. There wasn't a discussion or a resolution, just a quiet, silent, hauntingly uncomfortable calm that is best survived on that familiar shelf.

I don't like that aspect of me that learned to explode first. It is quite the opposite of the me that always gives in and gives up. I don't like that victim me either. Neither attitude is in any way, shape, or form healthy.

Tony Robbins' ten- or twelve-cassette series on personal power lived on the bottom shelf below our bedroom TV. I wanted to believe in what he taught: that to change a habit or create a new one, one must consciously be the change they want to achieve, intentionally, every day for at least thirty days. I needed to believe that habits can be changed.

Now there's a challenge, eh? Because I had mastered anger and the power of its energy, it became an ally, albeit not a good one. When anger reared its ugly face in my life, when it exploded out of me, I was the one who felt bad. I remember hitting my sister one afternoon when we were home alone. I was maybe ten, she was twelve. She wanted me to do something and I refused. I guess I was yelling so she put her hand over my mouth, and I swung. I went off to my room and cried. She wouldn't accept my "I'm sorry" and wouldn't tell me if I had hurt her. That was my first memory of exploding and I buried that ability until after years of living with anger, I let it out again.

As an adult my anger exploded with words, not fists. When I lost control of it, it blew out of me like a gale-force wind often, when I least expected it. It became a reactionary habit that left those in its wake unhinged, mistrusting, and feeling anything but safe. It was what I had come to use, not just as a last resort, but as a defense mechanism against the prospect of anger coming at me. Then it became my reaction to something that unhinged me or threw me off balance and it was almost always accompanied by tears.

I was good with words but the constant "trying to talk it out" never solved a thing. It takes two to have good communication and understanding in a conversation. At this point in my life, I was simply carrying on a conversation with me and myself. The mind games we can play with ourselves are often the very root of our own undoing.

Please understand that as I write this part of my journey and share all the emotion that comes up and bleeds out of me onto this page, I am not talking about physical violence. I am talking about an explosive energy manifested in words that spewed all over the room. I thought it a much healthier way to parent, to be vocally communicating, even in anger, as opposed to the quiet, scary stillness of the unspoken anger I grew up with. Imagine how I felt decades later when television commercials began to appear showing children crying on staircases as they listened to their parents argue. Another layer of guilt added to the growing pile as I didn't measure up to the standards of perfection I perceived from the "voices" of others.

The time had come. I first had to acknowledge that something had to change. Knowing something and acknowledging it feels like two completely different things to me. As I mentioned, I already knew I was not living in a way that filled my home or myself with joy; I already knew my family wasn't either, but I had never truly acknowledged it.

In constantly solving their problems, I was actually disempowering them. I was robbing them of their experience, of their opportunity to learn problem-solving or to face the consequences of forgetfulness or lack of responsibility. I was taking their power away from them.

I never realized how terrifying or unsettling it was for my husband, who had no clue where our money was or how it was spent. His checks went into the bank and I wrote the money out. Many years later, I would turn the bills over to him and let him see how it all worked, how to rob Peter to pay Paul and juggle the dollars from one place to another. He only lasted nine months, but to this day, he knows how hard that job is when there is barely enough and always a need for more as life grows up around us.

"In the face of unfair, we carry on, holding our breath and bracing ourselves, and only sometimes forgetting that there's always another storm right around the corner. They'll hit you, the storms, knock you off your moorings and send you overboard, desperate for anything to hold onto, to reel you up towards some semblance of peace. But life, I find is often more about the storms than the peace they seek to overwhelm. They look ready, any minute now, to shake things up and take your breath away."

–Tom Hanks in Road to Perdition

As life often showed me, I was living in an unbalanced way. A good friend exploded all over my world and was gone. My husband and son exploded all over each other and quit talking. My son left our home, and though I kept in touch with and saw him, he and my husband didn't speak for seventeen months.

At the time, I believed the rift between Danny and Ryan was the hardest thing I would ever be put through; in fact, it would prove to be simply an exercise for new life muscles I would need to strengthen in the years to come. All our family members and friends had an opinion or took sides. I can only imagine what my son's girlfriend's family thought of us or what stories they heard. I was angry and hurt and felt totally let down by my world; the one I had tried so hard to make work for everyone else proved to be completely broken for me. My daughter was away at college and I'd never felt so alone as I did then, even in a room full of people. Life became about just clicking off the days and, of course, staying extra busy.

Thankfully, the old adage that "Time heals all wounds" would find its way into our lives, with the help of our wonderful friend, Will. He got Danny and Ryan to a dinner table and the beginning of a new relationship, one they would grow into as adults instead of just father and son. They became best friends, my husband, and my son, and for that, I will always be grateful.

I, on the other hand, was still dealing with all the stuffed anger that was showing up in the circumference of my waist. Late nights were my time, no kids around, no husband with a remote (he goes to bed with the chickens and gets up with the rooster). It was my time to veg out in my big chair, control the remote and "stuff" my day with whatever jumped out of the refrigerator or freezer. No one was watching and I was ignoring that not-so-still voice in my head shouting, "*STOP IT! This is just another way to shove yourself back up there on that shelf!*" The heavier I got (not just physically, but energetically), the harder it was to get off the shelf.

"*It's okay,*" I would reply, "*Tomorrow I'll get that walk in and work it off.*"

"*Yeah, right!*" the monkey mind replied, "*It's just another day, another dollar, another aggravation, sad memory, more disillusioned thoughts fed, leading to more pounds.*" Ever have trouble deciding which voice to listen to, the loudest or the wisest? The loudest is the one that tells you about you, the wisest tells you what to do about you.

"*What happened to all this work I am doing in the mystery school?*" I would think and turn back the pages. "*Where has all the balance gone... again?*" I had just started to learn about mastering all these aspects of myself as a fourth-year apprentice in Lynn's school when my life exploded and blew me right out of my wheelhouse with the loss of our son.

Even now, as I stir up these buried memories, I want to feed them with ice cream and a good movie. My stomach tightens and I want to run. My head pounds and I look for a chocolate bar to soothe the growing beast that wants me to stop rewinding this story and just stuff it back on the shelf, into that deep recessed place in my belly where it can grow to its heart's delight and my waistband's fright.

It would be so easy right now to get up off this chair and go for a walk. The wind is clamoring for my attention, knocking at the doors and windows, rattling the tree branches against the house. Just as strong as these familiar energies, however, is this story, pulling at me to stay. I am coming to recognize the "pull of distraction" and on a rare occasion like now, I am able to wrestle it to the ground and sit on it, then return to the story that is clawing its way out of that dark recess within to make space for "me" to return.

A Way Off the Shelf: Write Away the Angry Day

Take out a blank piece of paper (preferably mixed media paper, at least 8x10). Using any colored pen or pencil, chalk, or paint, write all the words of anger that you can pull out of you and spew them all over the paper. It is good to write big and write small. It is fine to overlap the words and scribble them together, even draw pictures or symbols of this energy. Just write out your anger and let the paper take it all.

When you feel like you have emptied out all the anger that has been distracting and embroiling you, set the paper aside. Give yourself permission to let it rest outside of you and take a moment to breathe in the comfort of anger-less you. Feel the softness of no anger. Relax into the beauty of you in this moment without anger.

Close your eyes now and breathe – deeply inhale through your nose and hold it for a few seconds, then slowly exhale through your mouth, releasing any residual tightness around the anger that you have turned out. Blow your breath of anger-less you up into the air around you, behind you and above you, to the left and to the right of you.

Inhale deeply once again, this time visualizing a beautiful pink and green swirling light spinning around you. See it gently enter your heart, filling it with light, peace and the power of love expanded. See this beautiful energy as a part of you and allow it to take up residence in all the places vacated by the energy of anger you have released. Exhale slowly and know that the Universe abhors a void. You inhale this loving light and do not give anger's energy a place to return. Fill up the void left by its departure with another deep, cleansing breath, and when you truly feel full, comfortable, at ease and anger-less, pick up your powerless page of words and give them a funeral. You may just tear it up or cut it up and throw it away or take a bigger step and burn it, bury the ashes, and let Mother Earth transform what you have released. Let her fertilize the beauty of new growth with all that you have let go.

Chapter Twelve

NAVIGATING REALITY

It's strange, this book that is stalking me.
It is coming from behind and yet,
it feels like it is laid out like a trail in front of me.
All the stories seem to mill about shouting for my attention.
I don't know which one to call on next.

ime... I have never considered time my friend, though I have come to realize that I am not a good friend to time either. I don't honor it, I forget about it, I allow myself to run short of it and often disregard it altogether. I am learning that time is not my enemy, but just a process of the mind. I am addicted to multitasking and I push time, all the time.

"Hey, remember we have a drop-dead deadline," Cathy reminds me yet again. She is the lead on a project I'm helping write. A bit anal and very precise with her calendar, Cathy hovers.

"Leave me alone," I answer scornfully. "You know I'll get it done. I always do and yes, probably at the last minute, but I'll get it done."

I've told her a million times, if you want me to do it, just tell me what you want, when you want it and then leave me alone. It would drive the average, organized person batty to watch me and it makes me crazy to be asked all the time, "Is it done?" I understand her frustration, but I've never let her down; it's just how I am and how I have always done this crazy dance with time. You'd think by now she'd *just trust my process and leave me alone.*

Real estate would prove to be my saving grace. The year 1990 was my take-off year. I got so busy that the business became the place I began showing up as the me I was in everyday life, rather than who I thought I should be as a Realtor. I dressed for me, in my colored jeans with shirts that always matched my boots. In the summer, it was Birkenstocks and my socks always matched my shirts. Blazers were dress-up for me and in my style, went well with the jeans. I began to relax into me as a real estate professional and the business began happening.

You see, the people I met in my business were now meeting the authentic me. As I realized more and more that I was worthy of abundance in my life, abundance flowed freely into it. I had made a pact with Spirit when I joined Lynn's school, to show up and be open to the help I had asked for. That meant showing up at the office, answering my phone when I would rather be in the pool, making those appointments and keeping them, no excuses. The more I did, the more the phone rang. I was gathering abundance, getting out of debt, and beginning to build a new relationship with my husband and family as the energy of a more balanced life grew.

I learned from Walter Sanford that life is not about real estate, that real estate is a part of life. He taught the importance of balancing the "F" words in our lives: Faith, Family, Fun, Finances,

Fitness, and Friends. As my Grandma Wolf said, "Life is all about what you make it with what you have to stir in the pot. Sweet or sour, the choice is yours."

At the same time, life had gotten harder. The kids were getting older, and they didn't need as much of me or my time, but they needed support and funding. They had chosen hobbies that would take them to success in high school and on to college, but both of them chose extracurricular activities that had to be fed, literally.

Ryan seriously picked up his ropes in junior high school; turned out, he not only loved it, he was also exceptionally good at it. No real surprise there – he had been swinging a rope since he was big enough to get on his rocking horse by himself. As a toddler, he would rope anything walking by or moving. He was the jokester in the family, always finding a way to make people smile. Laughter was just part of his daily routine. He roped with his dad and when he got better than Danny, Danny found Ryan coaches in the roping world to keep him getting better.

Ryan continued to rodeo and went on to qualify for the National High School Rodeo Finals and the Silver State Invitationals. I got a lot of opportunities to put my good camera to use, shooting pictures of all the different rodeo and roping events.

I remember one time when I was on the north side of an arena just before one of his events. I needed to be on the south side to get the best picture. He rode over and "picked me up" off the fence, riding me double behind his saddle to the other side of the arena where he dropped me off before his run started. Sweet memories.

Raney wanted a calf to show. She was about twelve when we got her a little dairy heifer which she named Daisy. Raney learned with Daisy how to groom and show cattle. They were the highlight of the live nativity scene one Christmas. During her four years in Future Farmers of America (FFA), Raney had a polled Hereford project. Each year she also chose another animal to raise for the fair. She had turkeys her first year and topped the sale at the fair with her entry, "Mo Money." She raised a lamb, Houdini, her sophomore year. It could escape every enclosure we built for it except the chain-link pen around the kennels. The next year it was Sir Loinalot, a big white hog. Though she loved them all, her favorite was always Sara, her first polled Hereford. They used to sleep together in the straw piles at the fairs. Raney raised the Junior Calf Champion at the CA State Fair her junior year and medaled with her FFA projects every year.

Raney's greatest passion, however, was horses, and they still are today. At five, she got her first horse, a Welsh Quarter cross named Popper. A parent couldn't dream up a better first horse for their child. He was her best friend, companion, and confidant. He would stand beside the fence and let her slide down his neck to ride.

She would tell me years later, "Mom, horses aren't a possession of the mind. They are an obsession of the soul."

Raney learned to judge horses in FFA and went on to be the CA State Light Horse Judging Champion. Her junior year of high school, the FFA judging team qualified for the American Junior Quarter Horse Association World Show in Texas. We did a great fundraiser. The girls worked at farmers' markets, sold barbequed tri-tip roasts and raffle tickets at the grocery stores. Between the four of them, they made enough to cover all their expenses. I was talking about the logistics of going (as one of the chaperones) when Raney found me one morning and declared that she didn't want me to go.

"There won't be anything for you to do there, and it isn't like you would be watching me do anything. I watch the horses show in each class and then I write a critique and defend my placement choices to a panel of judges in a closed room. I really want to do this on my own."

I was heartbroken. I'd been just as excited as the girls about going to Texas, but if that was what she wanted, to spread her wings, I would stay home. This was her gig.

They did great. The team came in fourth in the nation and Raney was the AJQHA Jr. World Champion Halter Judge and fourth-highest individual. The proudest moment for her dad was watching her walk off the plane carrying that AQHA trophy, I teared up with joy for her.

FFA was a wonderful experience for Raney and for me as well, watching her learn to set goals and see her attain them, something I had never been taught to do. We were so proud to stand in Kansas City and watch her walk across the stage and accept her gold key, the American Farmer Degree, the highest national award given to a member of FFA.

Getting into Colorado State University and judging on the collegiate level was the final goal from her high school years. With that accomplished, she went on to co-coach a Colorado 4-H horse judging team to a national title. What Raney dreams, she achieves. She is a role model for me – strong, independent, and brave. I am so proud to be her mom.

Something was working – the kids were succeeding in what was important to them – yet they were struggling as siblings and home was not a calm, quiet place. I managed very well to keep the outside world plates spinning but I was losing the battle on the home front.

Going back a few years, Ryan, then a senior in high school, started hanging out at my mother's house (after my dad passed). Then he started staying over occasionally to "finish his laundry." Ryan loved to dance, and he and my mom took ballroom dancing lessons together. He was good to work the "honey-do" list his grandma kept up. Then, one day, he just didn't come home. A day or two went by and no one called; he just didn't come home.

I was mortified and furious. My mother had let him move in with her and never bothered to have a conversation with me about how I felt about it. Yet I couldn't say a thing; Mom was grieving the loss of my father and Ryan, a codependent like myself, was doing what he could to help her. As it turned out, he thought he was helping me as well, eliminating the chance of conflict between him and his sister.

"Hey, Mom, it was better that way," he would share when he returned home a year later. "Raney and I would not be arguing around the house anymore. I thought that would make it better for you."

I stuffed those feelings of betrayal by my mom and sadness at the loss of time with Ryan, right up there on the top shelf along with my self-esteem as a parent. I sure wish those kids had come with an instruction book.

I was trying to do it all while my husband went to work every day, came home, rode the horses, watched TV, and went to bed at dusk. I on the other hand sent the kids to their rooms by nine or ten so I could have that little piece of the night to call mine, to "control the remote" and stuff the day away. My life was very pretty on the outside, but I was dying on the inside.

Sure, I thought I was doing it right, that I got it right. I thought I did it the way I was supposed to. Even today, I am being challenged to stand in my own truth, to stand in my place of centered power and know that while it may not have worked for everyone, I was trying. Guilt was beginning to be one of the biggest stones I was carrying around and I had to constantly remind myself that I was doing the absolute best I could with what I had at that time in my life, with "what I had to stir into the pot," as Grandma Wolf had put it.

A wave challenges the beach with every tide that rolls in. It challenges the beach-dwellers and the landlubbers. Catch me if you can, withstand the force of my flow, time after time, day after day and look how beautiful the beach is. Face your challenges each day and like the beach, welcome them, embrace them, learn from them, and move on. Today, I am open to the challenges that will come my way as I work to stay off the shelf and face them intentionally.

I realized it was going to be my choice to rebuild a relationship with my husband, that I had to take the time out to spend with him or we were going to eventually end up going down separate roads. We started "dating" again, with Friday afternoons set aside for movies or dinner together. He was retired and I was still working, and I loved it when he called and said, "I've made dinner, you don't need to stop and pick anything up," or "I'll go get dinner, what do you want?" Those were the special moments our relationship had been missing, thinking about one another when we weren't in the same room.

We were becoming friends, beginning to find things to talk about together. With the children moving towards their own independence, we were growing into the "we" I had dreamed of some thirty-odd years earlier.

Monday mornings were my time – no phones, TV or internet. I started scheduling this "me" time to do my work in the mystery school. When Danny retired in '03, I was just in my second year in the school. Sometimes he would go to the bookstore after his morning get-together at the coffee shop or he would take off for the day with Ryan. Once a month, I would take our Friday afternoons and the weekend off, along with my Monday morning. It gave us the opportunity to go watch Ryan rope or fly to Colorado and visit Raney. Sometimes we would just take a drive over to the eastern side of the Sierras. Danny loves the high mountain deserts and I love the mountains.

One of my sacred teachers, Don Oscar, wrote, "Let us remember so as not to become meaningless, let us forget so as not to go mad." My daughter wrote in a Facebook post, "You can't hide or avoid it, there is no long way around it… walk into your fear."

For me, the hardest thing to hear these days is all the blame being thrown about everywhere and by everyone, from kids on the playground to our country's leaders. Then we begin telling ourselves and our children, "Be careful"; "Don't go there or do that"; "Stay away from…"; "Be safe"; "Know where you are and who you are with"; and for sure, "Always keep in touch with someone so if there is trouble, help can get there sooner."

When we buy into fear it owns us. If fear is becoming your lifestyle, become fearless and you cannot be controlled. When you take responsibility for your thoughts, words, and actions, you become fearless. When you become fearless in your life, no one can metaphorically "kill" you, energetically take you apart or feed you to their chickens. You become an artist, a warrior, and the choreographer of your life. Invite those who support and guide you towards your higher purpose to join you on the journey. Choose how you want to navigate your reality.

Oh, in the sky to be floating free,

to just be, to be me

I look down and see

I've become a cloud, I'm free

Sailing over the velvet seas

of green on green

Look at me,

I'm up here please

I've turned into a puff

Floating on the breeze

Finally, free – free to be me!

A Way Off the Shelf: Meditate with a Cloud

My mom used to tell me to look up at the clouds. We would talk about what we saw there: sheep jumping over trees, elephants trumpeting and lots of cuddly bears. She was teaching me to scrye the clouds, though I doubt that was her intention. She was teaching me to pay attention and "see" things, not just be bored and blind to the world around me.

I first heard the term scrye at one of Lynn Andrews' events many years later, and that's when I understood what Mom had been showing me. Wikipedia defines scrying, also known by various names such as "seeing" or "peeping," as the practice of looking into a suitable medium in the hope of detecting significant messages or visions. The objective might be personal guidance, revelation, or inspiration, and through the ages, scrying in various forms has also been a prominent means of divination.

There was always a fire on Saturday nights at Lynn's annual public gatherings, and after watching the fire for symbols and messages (scrying the fire), the fire team placed wet juniper over the flames to create clouds of swirling smoke. Watching the smoke (scrying the billowing clouds) was another way to listen and look for messages and symbols from the sacred fire.

Find a quiet place where you can spend a few minutes for yourself, with yourself and take a journey to the sky. If you can be outside, that's great, but you can also sit by a window or simply imagine the sky in your mind.

This exercise can be done anywhere: sitting against a tree, leaning on a boulder, or snuggled in your comfy chair, lying in the grass or on your bed, whether you are indoors, outside, or traveling in your imagination. It can be done anytime you gift yourself a few minutes.

Take a deep breath and as you release it, let your body and your mind relax. Allow your thoughts to travel out into the endless expanse of sky where the clouds roam free, bounce about, drift along with the wind, and play. Take another deep breath and allow yourself to "feel" the expanse of endless possibility that lies out there among the clouds.

Feel yourself as light as a puffy cloud and begin to see yourself drifting up and up, high into those clouds, the white puffy ones, and the darker gray stormy ones, those edged with the crimson cast of sunsets or the pristine pink of a sunrise. Feel the peace of floating surround you as you drift above the hurried chaos and hustle of the world below. You are free to be at peace, in peace and with the peaceful surrounding of the clouds that are unaffected by the rushing world below them.

What cloud are you most attracted to? Is it dense or feathery? Does it billow high into the sky or stretch itself out across the landscape of blue? Are you confined by definitions and boxes, or have you freed yourself to float, billow, expand, drift, and play in your world? Do you have a question for the clouds you are drawn to?

The clouds passing in front of the sun cast a shadow below, not unlike the way the difficulties you face can overshadow your days. The sun waits for its moment to break through and shine, just as the shadows will drift on and disappear, allowing you to shine more brightly in the midst of your challenges.

Spend some time drifting and playing with the clouds whenever you need to gain a new perspective on an old situation, habit, or challenge. Allow the clouds to gently hold you as you explore and expand your ability to navigate your own reality, free of the confines and constraints of everyday expectations. Chart the course that allows you to see beyond the illusion of others dreams, to see the truth beyond that is yours.

When you are ready to float back to your tree or boulder, your chair or bed, pick up your journal and write. Write what you saw and heard with the sky and the clouds you met. Write about the illusions illuminated from the other side of the shadow and write the truth you found beyond the expectations of others and your own inherited beliefs.

Chapter Thirteen

GETTING AWAY TO SAVE MY SANITY:
THE ACT OF LETTING GO

Dark shadows hanging over me
Dark Shadows all around.
I see them, feel them, sense them,
I am bound.
Breaking free seemed easy,
Breaking free is just a choice.
Still attached, I can't flee,
The pull of lingering shadows
Holding me.

"Hey Chris," I yelled across the yard, "I need a getaway. Want to come with me for a drive? I need to get out of town and breathe with the trees for a while."

"Give me thirty minutes," she called back.

Do you have a place to go when you need to get away but maybe only have a couple of hours? Is there a special place in nature near you where you can go and sit for a bit?

We all need some place that feeds us emotionally and spiritually. It can be the corner in your library surrounded by the books you love. It might be under a tree in your yard where the birds sing or the squirrels chatter. It could be at Starbucks where the scent of your favorite coffee brings you to that centered place inside that holds all the love you have ever needed.

I go to a waterfall about an hour's drive from my house. For me, waterfalls are where God touches the earth; they hold the magic and mystery of Nature. This place holds a space of calm and reason for me where I see a world of wonder and watch others wonder about what they see. The "little people's" spirits live and play here, tickling my silly bone and bringing laughter back into my day.

In one of my trips to Hawaii, I had learned about the Menehune, the little people of the Islands, not unlike the fairy folk or leprechauns we hear stories about. I suppose they go by different names in different parts of the world. Our teacher there spoke often of the "little people" and the importance of honoring them as they, like the leprechauns, are a playful bunch and like to play tricks, hide things, and sometimes trip you up or make you stumble. Putting out treats at night or tossing goodies to them on our hikes was a way of honoring their presence on this sacred land. It is something I have come to do as a regular practice when I venture onto new ground. I make it fun and talk to the Spirits of that Place and let them know that I know and honor them.

Everyday life distractions keep me from that place of stillness where I can open to other possibilities or others' voices or listen for messages in the wind. The waterfall offers me a sanctuary away from those.

There is an amazing grotto area just above this special waterfall, one I have only hiked to on a couple of occasions. That visit with Chris stands out in my mind as an incredibly special remembering of the joy of laughter and of childhood abandon.

That day, Chris and I decided to check out what was above and beyond the places we normally hiked to or hung out in. We carefully walked along the moss-covered rocks that lay like a puzzle along the edges of one of the streams that fed the waterfall. At one point, the creek widened a bit and there was an old, downed log that fell across the water. It was covered in a lush, thick layer of greens, light and dark mosses. Lichens grew on the rocks in the shaded areas, like paint splatters on a board canvas in reds, pale yellows, and deep blue greens. The downed tree and surrounding branching and rocks created a grotto in a dead-end-like space where the water pooled, and light danced with the shadows across the tiny pond.

Chris and I found a couple of rocks to climb up on and we settled into a comfortable quiet, listening to the water trickle under the big log and across the rounded stones. A giddy feeling came over me and I looked around at Chris to see her smiling as well. Focusing back on the little flow of water and the moss-covered sticks and stones, a movement caught my eye. I stared for a bit, and as my gaze softened, I saw more movement and then a splash. I could hear giggles and laughter and then caught just the quickest glimpse of a tiny person running around a branch and jumping into the pool of water under the log. Of course, I blinked and tried to focus on a particular spot but when I did, I just saw the beauty of this place we rested in.

Remembering what one of my teachers had shared with me, I reached into my pocket and pulled out a handful of almonds tossing a few across the creek while whispering a soft greeting and "thank you" for allowing us to share this sacred space and play place. Tossing a few more nuts, I asked that "they" (the wee ones here) not play any jokes on us nor trip us up in our hiking.

I could hear again the laughter and sense the presence of whole families of little people jumping and playing in this magical space. There was a tiny rope swing hanging from a fork in the branch suspended over the pool. Watching, for what seemed like hours, just filled my heart with joy. It was as if in watching all their fun I was letting go of the heaviness that had brought me to the waterfall that day. I was inhaling their joy as my own. With the setting sun, the light in the grotto was fading and the little people were scurrying off the rocks and out of the trees and heading up a tiny trail the other side of the creek. Bringing my focus back into the present moment, I looked back at Chris. We laughed and shared the stories of the little people's antics as we had watched them.

One of the most important lessons I have learned in my studies is that what I imagine is real. It takes a bit of practice to truly embody this teaching, but it is of fundamental importance if you are to become your own spiritual authority (as another of my teachers, Beth Beurkens likes to say). I have come to truly trust this and that has opened me up to "seeing" whole new worlds. It was so fun sharing this adventure with someone who holds that same understanding and was able to "see" with her mind and her eyes. We were able to share the "fun" we watched and talk about the joy we encountered in that grotto.

Leaving carefully, watching to place our feet where we had not seen the little ones, Chris and I made our way back along the creek and down the hill toward Heart Falls. We spent some time with our feet in the water, consciously now, releasing anything that had come up for us that needed to be let go, giving it to the water to be washed away in its flow. This is a place of such majesty and strength, and it lends itself to inner peace.

Chris hiked out ahead of me and I spent a few minutes sitting cradled in the roots of an ancient pine tree growing in the banks of the creek below the falls. This Grandfather Standing Tall One has shared his wisdom with me through the years. His message to me that afternoon was to remember. I didn't need to make the hour's drive here to release the weight of my days. I could simply take a few moments in silence and run my own spiritual roots out through my feet, deep into the Earth, letting go of all that I was done with, knowing that the Earth could take all that heavy darkness that I felt enveloped by and transmute it into the light and beauty of places just like this.

I am reminded that all of life is an Act of Letting Go and here in this place I have dubbed Heart Falls for the shape of a spot worn in the rock, I can do just that. I put my feet in the icy water remembering that all is right in the world if I choose to see it that way. Joseph Campbell wrote that "The goal of life is to make your heartbeat match the beat of the Universe, to match your nature with Nature." That is exactly what happens for me at Heart Falls. It is here that I let go of my attachments to the mundane, the "ordinary," to other people's thoughts of who I am. It is here, in nature, that I take intentional, courageous action in my life. It is here, when I am off the shelf, that everything shifts.

I carry around a little piece of paper with a quote from Maya Angelou. It reminds me that normal isn't enough! She said, "If you are always trying to be normal, you will never know how amazing you can be!"

Amen!

A Way Off the Shelf: Listening to a Tree

You may live in the city, the suburbs or out in the country. Chances are, wherever you are, you can see a tree. One of my earlier teachers, Margaret Hudson, shared a story with us at art camp many years ago. Margaret was an older woman, white-haired and soft-spoken when I met her, and well-known in our area for her amazing art and clay animal statues and figures. At one time, her paintings lined hospital corridors and her unique moon-eyed sculptures filled gardens and gift shops all over California and the surrounding states.

In her story (I remember parts of it and will fill in the rest), she shared how she needed a getaway and rented a small cabin up in the mountains. She planned to draw, maybe paint, and read in the quiet of a mountain retreat. When she got to the cabin, she was so disappointed to find the picture window view in the front room, was almost totally obstructed by a giant redwood tree. Its massive trunk was nearly as wide as the window itself. Margaret's intended peaceful view to fill her days had become one of irritation and aggravation. She tried moving the chair around to get at least a partial view of the mountain, with little luck. On her second day there, feeling a bit more at ease, she opened the window. The scent of cedar, pine and manzanita filled the stuffy cabin with fresh mountain air.

Margaret is one of those women who has faced unthinkable grief: the loss of a son. She transformed the powerful emotions of her grief into art. Sitting in that chair by the window, her attention was drawn to the tree. Laughing to herself as only Margaret could, she focused her attention on that tree. She began drawing the patterns of the bark on her sketchpad. As she did, words began drifting into her consciousness and she found herself writing them along the veins of the bark she was drawing. Imagine wavy, flowing lines intersecting each other in curves and dead ends as the design of the redwood bark filled her page. In the spaces between and along these lines, words began appearing and a story unfolded. Margaret wrote the messages from that tree in the crisp mountain morning air and tucked them into her memory.

Truth be told, she was listening to the tree. It took the frustration of that blocked window to move through her, taking the chaos of her life with it. It smoothed the way for her to find the reason she needed to get away. She surrendered to the moment and relaxed into this quiet space, doing what she did to bring herself into joy. She created art. In that space of silent joy, she was open to hearing another voice in the language of the trees and she listened.

When I find myself stuck, frustrated but unable to go to the mountains or the park or take a drive and get away, I find a tree. I have been blessed to have some beautiful and profoundly wise ones living on our property. I would just walk outside and be in the presence of those trees. When I could without interruptions, I would sit beneath one and work to find that space of silence within that allowed me to hear a Voice other than mine. I would take a journal, and when I was out of my own way, I could write with the voice of the trees, their messages moving me out of my need to get away and allowing me to move back into my everyday world more relaxed and at ease.

Try this sometime – you might be surprised at the wisdom these Standing Tall Beings have to impart. Walk out in your yard, a community park or just down the street. You don't have to live in the country, perhaps you live in a multi-storied building. If you look out your window, you can probably see a tree. Whether sitting with one or looking to one in the distance, send your intent, your focused thoughts, out to that tree. Sit with it or by your window, look up into its branches and leaves, watch it, be still and listen.

An easy way to begin journaling is to simply write what you see; the tree, the colors, the movement of the leaves, the people, or animals near it. Listen for the language of that tree to speak to you and keep writing. Have fun and explore. Sometimes the getaway you need is just outside your window.

Chapter Fourteen

I AM ALL I NEED TO BE

Doubt quivers in the bottom of my stomach
My hands are cold while my forehead sweats.
It creeps in between rainbows in nighttime dreams,
Yet fails to go away with the sun.
Doubt has a stranglehold on my imagination,
Bleeds all over inspiration,
Quelling thoughts of exploration until I raise a fist to Doubt.
I vanquish it from reality,
Replace it with new certainty,
Filling my consciousness with fresh awareness
I AM ALL I NEED TO BE!

"Hey, Mom," I heard a voice call down the hall, "You up?" I tried to ignore it. I had no desire whatsoever to get up. Let me just lie here quietly and maybe they'll go away.

"Hey, Mom!" the voice grew more anxious, "You Okay?"

There was no ignoring that plea. "I'm fine, honey, just tired this morning. Do you need something?"

Silence followed my answer…

Rumi called it, "You've seen my descent. Now watch my rising."

I have fought depression my entire life. It wasn't something we talked about when I was younger, or ever really until much later in my life. My mother told me, simply, that it was up to me to pull myself up by my bootstraps and get on with it. After all, "It is the woman's place to set the tone in her family."

I thought my mom had it all together. Our home was well kept, and I don't really remember feeling a lack for anything. Mom did a great job at covering up what wasn't working in her life and just getting on with it.

Long before losing our son, I shrank to the kitchen floor one evening and simply thought, "I can't do this anymore." I couldn't decide what to make for dinner and worried it wouldn't be right for someone. My husband just said, "What have you got?"

"Really," I replied, "I'm supposed to stand in front of the refrigerator and read labels 'til something sounds good to you?"

Nobody answered.

Our daughter was a picky eater, to put it mildly; our boy would eat most anything (though he wasn't a fan of tuna casserole). Who would I disappoint with whatever decision I made for dinner that night? I just slid to the floor, down the face of the cabinet in the corner of the kitchen, knowing I was done. I couldn't play this self-imposed guessing game anymore. There would never be the right answer for everybody. I wasn't strong enough in my own beingness to say, "This is what's for dinner tonight!" without that nagging, gut-burning doubt that I wouldn't get it right.

It was time to seek help. I went to my medical doctor first and Gene told me I had three choices. I could see a psychiatrist (expensive), a psychologist (moderately costly) or a minister (generally free). I chose the minister to begin with and not being active in a church at that time, he sent me to his Mennonite minister, for a chat.

Having young children, running a home business, and trying to keep up with everything that I thought was expected of me, had buried me under a pile of expectations that I felt I was not living up to. Guilt had become a constant companion. I was working from home, showing dogs, coaching our daughter's softball team, was team mom and scorekeeper for our son's baseball team, trying to keep house and do the bookkeeping, feed horses, dogs, kids, and cattle, oh yes and hubby too. I also had to manage whatever needed to be handled at any given moment.

It never felt like I had any backup, but truth be told here, master little co-dependent that I had become, I never asked for help from anyone (except sometimes my mother). It was often more trouble than it was worth because our family communication skills were far from good. I was trying to figure out how to keep all the plates in my life spinning in the air and some were getting pretty darn wobbly. Before they fell, I asked for help.

The minister crushed my perception of what I thought I should be doing by telling me that my priorities were all out of order. It was my job first and foremost to put God first, then my husband and children next and then... me? Not sure what all else fell into the space of those dots; I got lost in the idea that I was letting everybody down by not putting them all first when in my world, I thought I was. Please, let me get back up on that shelf where I can exit the scene, let life go by and not be responsible for it. This wasn't working. I went home to sell my show dogs, clean up my house, find my family a church and get back on the right track.

I called my doctor back and asked for that referral to the psychologist. My mother had agreed to pay for whatever the insurance wouldn't cover as grooming dogs wasn't going to. I had to find those damned bootstraps mom had told me about so I could pull myself back up and get on with it, get "life" right this time.

I found a friend in the psychologist I was referred to. Each week for years, nearly ten of them in fact, I showed up and told her all the things I did and what had happened since our last visit. My medical doctor put me on medication when I had an anxiety attack. Yep, dog groomer now working in someone else's shop and paying them for the privilege. I had given up my show dogs, closed the kennels and gone to work in town. We converted the kennel into a one-bedroom guest house and rented it. That rent paid the ranch utilities and hay bill. Grooming was a job that bought the groceries, paid for game uniforms, and allowed me the flexibility to still be home for the kids after school. At that time in our lives, the real estate thing was not working out for me.

Doing all of this was the smarter thing to do for everyone, or so I thought then. Once again, "Vicki" was exiting the scene in favor of shelf life while life just kept on moving. The advantage was that I was making money every day and not really spending it. We called it the "grocery and extras" money. My husband had a good job and certainly provided all we needed to live, but I thought there was so much more and wanted so much more for my kids whose hobbies were far beyond a ballpark. They were getting involved with horses, our son rodeoing and our daughter beginning with FFA and livestock projects. All our hobbies now had to be fed, not just looked after.

About the time I thought I was getting things into perspective, digging into deeper conversations, beginning to do more than just talk about all I did each week, Gail up and moved to Colorado. I began seeing her partner in the office, a man named Bill. He had a completely different point of view, and within weeks I was seeing that what I was doing, the way I was being, wasn't healthy for anyone and was killing me.

He told me to look up the word no in the dictionary and learn how to master it. He helped me get off the anxiety drugs, though the psychiatrist he sent me to wanted to replace them with different meds specifically for depression. When one didn't seem to have any effect, there was a different one prescribed. I repeatedly said, "I don't think they are doing a darn bit of good." I sure couldn't tell any difference even after the third "flavor." I remember being at a real estate mastermind event in LA with more samples of yet another drug to start after this two-week trial ended. I remember flushing them all down the toilet (sorry, my bad, I didn't know any better then). Why am I taking stuff and not feeling any better? I also noticed that my conversations with the counselors had become an outlet for the "stories" I couldn't tell anywhere else. That said, Bill had given me some surprisingly good advice and gotten me off meds; he had also shown me a different point of view, one that gave me permission to put me, my wants, and my needs into the equation. The problem was, I had no clue how to put that into practice.

173

Life simply went on for me as it always had, living on the shelf with maybe a glimpse of what could be, but no concrete means to incorporate it into my reality. I had aging parents to begin thinking about caring for, a thriving real estate career with a constantly ringing phone, kids heading off to college and a looming empty nest with a husband I had grown away from, as he had me. He was a Scorpio, okay being alone. Being a Gemini, I wasn't. He was the epitome of the Willie Nelson song where he tells us mamas not to let our babies grow up to be cowboys, cause they're always alone, even with someone they love. I remember telling him one chilly evening sitting on the edge of the fireplace, "Either we get to be friends again or I'm out of here when our daughter leaves for college. I'm not going to live in a house with someone else to do for and worry about and still be alone."

For the first three years of my real estate career, I lived on Benadryl, staving off the hives as I tried to do it all. If you said real estate to me, I broke out in welts, big lumpy ones not just little rashes. You see, as far as I could tell, buyers were liars, sellers never told the truth and FSBOs (for sale by owner) ate their young. I had no training in the business, real estate school taught the test, not the business. I didn't understand or even have a clue about the foundational work it took to become successful in the real estate industry. I just showed up at office meetings, heard about everyone else's business, and answered the phones when it was my turn. The first broker I hung my license with didn't offer any training, but she was there to answer questions, if only I had a clue what questions to ask.

Things changed for me in late 1989, when a broker from another company sold my only listing. I told him I was going to quit because it was too much stress and I had only closed five transactions in my three-plus years in the business. Alvin encouraged me and insisted I could be good. He told me I returned calls and showed up when I was supposed to. He (Mr. Togo) recruited me to his office and with much trepidation, I agreed to move, still thinking I would let my license expire in July 1990. I didn't know we were in a market boom at that point in time.

Alvin ran informational and educational office meetings. I began to learn what the business of real estate involved. I realized that I should be marketing me. I went to classes and seminars. I learned how to sell "me," not just houses, and I got exceptionally good at it. I loved marketing, especially outside the box that most real estate agents were in. I had closed my kennel and grooming business and was working in someone else's shop while trying to learn the real estate business. With Alvin's help and encouragement, I groomed my last dog on Valentine's Day 1990.

I had found something I was good at, that made real money and it was perfect for the people-pleasing skills I had mastered since childhood. More important than even the money, I found a place to work that let me begin to be "me" as a Realtor, where, as I mentioned earlier, I could wear jeans and Birkenstocks or roper boots. I relaxed into me and met clients as the same authentic me they might run into on the ballfield or in the grocery store. I was learning that I could be successful as Vicki, not playing the role I thought Vicki should be playing. I got involved in our community and my world lightened up. I was walking through a self-driven life instead of a reactionary one. I was finding my way off the shelf, conquering doubt; I just hadn't realized it yet. It would be near the end of the nineties when I began to realize there was more to me than just being needed; I was going to learn that I already had and was all I ever needed.

A Way Off the Shelf: Mirroring You to You

This is my adaptation of an exercise done in Writing Spirit, the School, by Lynn V. Andrews.

Find a mirror (preferably a full-length one) and "see" yourself standing in front of that full-length mirror under the soft glow of a white light. Take in this softly illuminated reflection of YOU... All of you from top to toes. Do you recognize YOU?

You must be familiar with this reflection; you have seen it a million times in your own mirrors, in the reflections of your memories, passing glassed in storefronts, puddles in the rain and newly washed cars. You see the shapely curves and crevices of your shadowed outline and you remember YOU.

"Wait, what?" The light goes out but the negative image of you is still in front of you standing in the mirror, a shadowy reflection of the you, you were just looking into. "What's going on?" you wonder out loud as you try to focus on your shadowed self.

Close your eyes and "look" again. You want to see you, remember that familiar form, those eyes, that smile that was familiar to you just moments ago. Can you see you, or are you fading without the light?

Squint your eyes tighter and look deeper into the void left in the dark. See things you may not have seen before. Open your eyes and look, look harder, look deeper into the dark.

"OW!"

You cover your eyes as the light pops on so bright in the darkness and now look! There YOU are again. You can still see the "shadow" of you remaining around the edges of this you, flashbulb you, that is reflected back at YOU.

"Yes! There I am!" You shout, seeing you again. Just as you come into clear focus, poof, the light goes out, leaving you struggling once more to recapture, remember the image you were looking at even as the darkened (like a photographic negative) image of your reflection begins to appear as a now-familiar shadow figure of you. As you begin to focus on this shadow, this negative-like image of you, poof! The light comes back on again!

How is your mind reacting? What is your bodymind (the mind in the center of you) trying to tell you? Are you attached to one or the other of the images, or more attached to a memory of an image of you?

Looking beyond your reflection in the mirror, you see a chair against the wall behind you. You step backward in this "on" light, not taking your eyes off the mirror, and sit down. You are now facing the reflection of you sitting in this chair.

Which one are you? Are you both? Are you seeing a different characteristic of you that is still you, seeing you?

Take out your journal and pen as you sit in the comfort of your own reflection and write this journey you took – seeing you watching you, looking at you, seeing You.

Did you see the same "you" in the light that showed up in the dark?

Was the shadow you, or just around you?

Was your reflection changed when the light came on, or was it the same as when it went off?

Play with this exercise, have fun with it, write it light and write it dark, write in beauty and write the shadow. This is you searching for you…. WRITE YOU seeing that you are all you need to be!

Chapter Fifteen

PUTTING YOU FIRST

Egos circle negative energy abounds.
Women gathering two by two.
Desert energy surrounds
The balance upset with the entry of third.
Suddenly it's crowded and tempers run free.
Where is there space for me to be me?
I'm stuck right there in the middle.
Who to please and how to be me?

"*L*et's go, let's go!" she shouted as she bounded around the corner of the tent. Elaina had been napping after their noon meal, under a tree down by Chilkoot Creek, not a stone's throw from the campsite. She hadn't been watching the time and it had gotten away from her.

This is one of my stories, an experience that taught me a lot about allowing me to put me first. I've changed the names and the historical timing, but the lesson is the same…

It was time for their first meeting at the annual Stone Creek

Gathering. Marni wasn't ready, she was moving slowly this afternoon. Elaina and Genise started off without her.

"Oh wait!" Marni yelled, "I'll just be another minute."

Frustrated by the delay but feeling like it was important to be together, Elaina and Genise waited while Marni finished getting ready. They made their way to the central meeting place and quietly took their places in the back of the room filled with women waiting, singing, and drumming in anticipation of their teacher's arrival. Winded from the last-minute rush, Elaina found it hard to quiet down and concentrate. Several deep breaths later, she vowed softly to herself not to be distracted from the days ahead. This is the annual meeting of her people. They come to listen and learn, to journey for power and to meet themselves in the process.

The girls, Elaina, Genise and Marni, had met at this event the year before. They had run into each other searching for a place to set up camp and decided it would be easier to camp together in one large tent rather than separately in small ones by themselves. They all lived in the western part of the country – one by the ocean in the north, one in a valley centrally located between the other two, and the third in the desert to the south. They shared the love of this gathering and the things they learned there and had made plans to "room" together again this year.

The first meeting ended as evening came and it was time for dinner. Everyone would gather around a central fire area and share in a buffet-style meal. The three girls made the hike back to their campsite to get ready. They changed their clothes, washed up and gathered the food they had brought to share. Elaina had been wearing sandals with her denim skirt and more than once had stubbed her bare toe on the rocks along their path.

"We should change quickly and get back," Elise said, trying to motivate the other two to get a move-on. Putting on her soft leather boots, she reminded Marni and Genise, "You know how fast the food goes. If we are late, we will just have leftovers to pick through for dinner."

Marni was busy redoing her flaming red hair and Genise was packing food.

"We have plenty," Marni scoffed back as she went to change her skirt. She loved being "seen" and wore bright colors made into flowing skirts that bounced around her when she danced about the campus. Genise and Elaina both dressed in simple fashions, although Genise always wore beautiful jewelry, big silver earrings and a necklace that usually matched her clothes.

"I'm ready," Genise called out as she carried the bundle of food out to Elaina's wagon.

It is a hike back to where the girls have set up their tent. Elaina had driven her wagon this year, remembering how long it took to cross the campgrounds last year. She asks her friends if they would like a ride and of course they echo their yeses in the evening quiet.

The girls worked together to hitch the wagon to Elaina's little pony Jilly, and they head off to dinner, laughing as they bounced over rocks scattered over their path.

Someone's dog bounds up and jumps into the wagon with the girls, then out again as it sees a rabbit across the field and takes chase. Giggling together, Elaina asks Jilly to hurry it up a bit as she gently slaps the reins across the pony's fanny in encouragement.

So many people have gathered this year, there must be one hundred and fifty, maybe two hundred people all milling around the evening fires visiting and nibbling and enjoying this first meal they were sharing all together.

Elaina left her friends and joined a group of girls she hasn't seen since last year. They laughed and talked and ate, catching up on the past year before going on to the night meeting together.

When this late meeting was over, Elaina looked around for Marni and Genise but couldn't find them anywhere. She got in her cart and drove her little black pony slowly back to the eating area, hoping to find them. No one had seen them since supper, so Elaina headed back to their tent.

Shortly after she had settled in for the night, Marni and Genise showed up, tired and a bit upset with her for not waiting around to give them a ride back to their tent. Elaina explained that she did wait and had looked for them. She told the girls that she even went back to the eating area and couldn't find them. The three agreed that they would meet at the big eucalyptus tree on the far side of the eating area after meals each day and go together to their meetings. Elaina grumbled quietly under her covers.

"I'm not waiting. If they don't show up on time, I'm just going to get myself to the gatherings alone."

The voice in her head was telling her differently, telling her she would give in and wait anyway, knowing she wouldn't want to disappoint them even if it made her late.

She sighed and drifted off into a restless sleep. Now she was tied down to being a shuttle service for her friends. When would she have the time to explore, to visit her other friends, to sit in silence in this wonderful place, on this sacred land at their Stone Creek Gathering? Her sleep was restless that night, fitful and filled with unremembered dreams.

The next morning the three women were up with the sun and took a quick dip in Chilkoot Creek – a little, quieter stream of water that branched off the river known as Stone Creek. The waters of Chilkoot formed a natural pond just below an eight-foot waterfall spilling over giant boulders and piles of rocks. It was the perfect place to bathe or swim or just be in the water. Elaina recharged herself in the pool. Water always brought her back to a sense of balance, a place of remembering herself with the water's unconditional support. This morning she needed it, she was tired from her lack of sound sleep and there would be so much to do today. She allowed herself a few extra minutes to just float and release her tension to the water, relaxing into that floaty place from which she could just drift away and "be" in the moment.

Back at their campsite, the three girls loaded the wagon, hitched up Jilly and headed off to breakfast. Elaina and Genise took their packs and all they would need for the first meeting that morning and for lunch as well. Marni hurried out of the tent at the last minute and joined them as the wagon began to roll down the dirt road to breakfast.

Marni was winded and again agitated that Elaina and Genise had not waited for her. They tried to explain that they were not going to wait anymore, that if Marni wanted to ride to the eating fires area or even to the meeting flats, she would have to be ready when they were or walk there on her own.

Elaina hated confrontation and the ride to breakfast was one wrapped in uncomfortable silence. She left Jilly tethered to the eucalyptus tree near where they ate and wandered off by herself carrying her pack in readiness for the morning gathering. She wanted to get there early and find a good place to sit where she could see and hear her teacher. Today she promised herself, she would take whatever time she needed to get the most out of this gathering.

The day went well. Elaina had taken care of herself, done what she wanted, when and where she wanted without giving up her time worrying about her companions. Sunset was approaching. Elaina hadn't seen Genise or Marni all day. She decided to get her pony and ride to a hilltop to watch the sun set this evening. She felt the need to sit alone in silence and voice her gratitude for the day's lessons. She unhitched Jilly and just as she was riding away from the cooking fires, she heard someone yelling her name. She turned and it was Marni running after her.

"Where are you going?" she inquired, "Can I come along?"

Reluctantly but again unable to say no, Elaina waited while Marni caught up and climbed up behind her on Jilly. Silently arguing with herself, Elaina grumbled, *"Why can't I just say no? I hate it when people look disappointed or upset with me. Then I feel bad, get upset with myself. My insides just churn all around the 'yes', making it so uncomfortable for me, but I say yes anyway."*

When they arrived at the top of the hill, Marni jumped down, began gathering stones and setting up a sacred circle, calling in the directions and waiting on Elaina to join her. Elaina brought her drum and a small flute, respectfully entering their circle. She sat down, faced the setting sun, closed her eyes, and began to play, letting her mind drift with the song her flute sang. Marni interrupted and asked her to drum while she danced the sun down singing her own song, the words unknown to Elaina.

With a deep sigh and a knot twisting in her belly, Elaina put down her flute, picked up her drum and began to rhythmically tap out a cadence for Marni to dance to. Even Elaina's drum was not happy and voiced her discomfort with a tight, twanging, tinny sound. All Elaina could think about was why she had said yes to Marni's request to come along in the first place.

The evening didn't turn out to be anything at all like she had imagined. As the sun set in the west silhouetting the trees and the cactus across the dusty desert hills, Elaina vowed to herself that she would learn how to say no without guilt. She had overheard a couple of new girls talking at their last meeting.

"Why can't people just make up their minds and say yes or no," one of them asked. "I watched the craziest thing at dinner. There was this group that kept pushing one of the girls to do something she didn't want to do. You could tell how uncomfortable she was. She kept trying to say no, but the others weren't hearing her. They just pushed back saying to her, "It'll be okay," or "Just this time." Things like that."

"Too many people won't take no for an answer without causing a big scene," the other girl answered. "And if you don't stand up for yourself, you'll just get walked all over."

Such a perfect message for me to overhear tonight, Elaina thought. *I'm going to practice boldly standing up for me, stating my own wants and needs firmly, and I will hold tighter to my own personal boundaries. No more giving in to the constant barrage of requests and demands from others.*

It would take a lot of practice to change this habit of setting herself aside with a yes when for her the no would be better. She would learn to put herself first.

The last day of the gathering had arrived. Elaina and Genise had earlier agreed to get up before dawn to walk out into the desert to watch the sunrise. Marni heard them stirring and sat up and ask if she could come along. Elaina let out a sigh and a weak, "Fine."

Genise firmly answered, "If you can be ready to go right away! We are leaving in just a few minutes. We are not going to miss the rising sun."

Elaina and Genise finished packing their backpacks and were heading for the tent flap when Marni exclaimed, "Wait, wait, I am coming!"

Genise shouted back that they were not waiting any longer and, taking Elaina by the arm she led her out of the tent. Elaina was consumed with guilt almost immediately and questioned Genise about them not waiting just a bit longer for their friend.

"Do you want to see the sun rise?" Genise asked. Elaina nodded her head yes. "Then we must go!" It was that simple. "We have given in to her tardiness all week and I am not going to do it anymore. If you want to give up the sunrise to wait for her, go ahead. I'm not, I am leaving." With those words, Genise flipped the tent's flap back and stomped out.

Elaina thought for about half a second, then quietly thanked Genise for showing her what taking control of her own time was all about. The two of them set off across the desert in the bluish-gray dawning of this last morning they would have together for another year.

They found a rocky hill just made for climbing and picked their way to the top in time to see the sky change from dark blue-gray purples and pink to firelight orange as it fades into the soft blue sky of dawn. The shadows of the rocks below them began to stretch out as they crawled across the sandy ground with the rising sun. The desert took on a pastel blanket of pink and peachy hues that quickly turned to golden shades of amber then yellow as the sun climbed over the hills and into the Eastern sky. What a magnificent play of colors and shadows, which Elaina would have missed had she waited a minute more for Marni.

Elaina and Genise planted prayer sticks on the top of the hill. They had decorated them with pieces of ribbon and woven blades of grass collected at the campsite around the sticks. With Genise singing softly in the background, Elaina spoke aloud, "I vow to take back the power to control my time. I have given it away to all the people in my life. No more! I accept responsibility for my own actions, for those yes decisions when I wanted to say no and realize that in waiting on others to share my experiences, I am diminishing my own." She let out a long sigh, knowing this was a big step in her life, one she thought was worth taking.

The rising sun cast a shadow westward from the prayer sticks they had just planted. Elaina felt a death deep within her, the passing of this need she had lived with for so long, this need to please others and make sure they were happy for her to enjoy, or perhaps validate her own experiences. She envisioned that lengthening shadow carrying away her need for other people's happiness to be her burden. Without thinking, she pulled the bone-handled knife from its sheath on her belt and made a slashing movement through the shadow of her prayer stick even as it began to shrink with the rising sun.

Elaina looked over at Genise standing quietly in the morning light, a smile spreading across her face. "Way to go, my friend!"

That morning in the newness of the rising sun, she had found, within herself, a place of welcoming awareness that she was all she needed. A knowing that within her was all she had been, was now, and would ever be.

Elaina placed her hand over her heart and then waved it palm up and outward towards her friend Genise, signaling her heartfelt gratitude for mirroring to Elaina the strength she had within her own self.

Facing the now-risen sun, Elaina bowed in thanks then raised her arms in gratitude for the beauty of this unfolding day and the two friends who had been her greatest teachers at this year's gathering.

Elaina and Genise made their way back to the final meeting with their teacher and farewells with all the family of friends they'd come together with that year. Elaina was taking home with her a newly remembered piece of herself that she'd given away long ago. The year to come would be a new experience that Elaina would face with herself, by herself and for herself. As she moved to hitch up Jilly for the ride home, she saw a small, pinkish-red stone lying beside the wheel of her cart. She put it in her pocket, knowing she would place it somewhere special at home, remembering, each time she saw it, the beautiful sunrise that gifted her such a powerful message and her dear friend who had reminded her it was okay to say no.

The story of Elaina and her experience at the Stone Creek Gathering is the truth of one of my own experiences at a retreat. I changed the time, place and names to create this little "teaching story." I realize in retelling it here that it in those times of saying yes when I want to say no, when the shadow dwellers push forth all their negativity, they are telling me that it is time to get out of the situation, whatever story I'm telling myself, write out the characters that no longer serve a loving and supportive role in my life, and write in new characters, lessons, and teachers; to put me first.

I can feel underqualified and overwhelmed, struggling under too many expectations, my own and those I perceive others have placed on me. The weight of it all would bury me when I didn't remember I matter, that I must take care of me, to put me first, and keep the key to my toolbox close at hand.

A Way Off the Shelf: Sacred Art

My "take care of me" toolbox contains tips and tricks, ceremonies, and celebrations for finding my way back to me when I get lost, thrown off track, or find myself giving me away in too many places. I come back to "Vicki" with some form of creativity.

In this powerful and fun exercise, I share below, I can take my feelings, the ones keeping me heavy or sad, and move them out of me. I release them through an act of creating.

This is what I like to call Sacred Art. I start by lighting a candle and taking a few deep breaths, allowing my body to relax and my mind to let go of whatever is happening around me. In whatever manner you call in the Infinite Intelligence that surrounds you, let your intent be known and create an aura of divine love and protection around you. Only what is right and perfect for you in this moment will enter.

I get out a big blank piece of art paper (I like mixed media) heavy enough to paint and write layers on. I gather up some tissue paper, watercolors, and acrylics, cut pictures and words out of old magazines and catalogs and I pull out the Sharpie markers.

I take out the old envelope I keep filled with cut-up scraps of paper. I will write these three words on separate pieces of paper – Me, Family, Life.

Then I spontaneously think of three more words, the darker, the better. Maybe they are inspired by the first three words – I don't think about them; I just write the first three "dark and heavy" words that come to mind. I don't wait and I don't ruminate, I write.

There is no right or wrong! If you are doing this for yourself, take all six little papers and put them into a pile or an old cup or fold them and toss them on a paper plate. See, there are no rules here – there is just you, doing something for you.

Continuing, I pull the first word, read it out loud, and write it somewhere on my "canvas." I then begin to paint, scribble or write whatever colors, symbols, words or messages come from this first word. I paint beauty or I paint ugly, I don't think, I just do. You can use your markers, draw hearts, use your paint, and splatter monsters, pull out your hair, even spit on the paper. This is the energy of this first word moving out of your body and your mind into a physical creation. You are letting the energy of it go...

When you feel complete with this first layer, this first word, take a piece of tissue paper (plain or glittered, color doesn't matter) and tear it in pieces. You can plaster them all over the wet surface you have just created or simply plop them in spots, follow your intuition and stay out of your mind. Use them to cover parts of the page or smear them around or create textures and let the wet layer bleed into and around the tissue. If it gets too dry, and you still want to play, spray it with water.

When you feel done, let it dry then repeat this process with each of the remaining words. Pick a word and draw, write, paint, spatter, glue, tape and create right over the first dried layer... just keep adding to this piece, word after word. You are forming a physical manifestation of your thoughts and feelings, the dark and the light, moving the dense, the heavy and the sad out of you as you fill up with the light and joy of creativity.

When you are all finished, when you feel complete with the entire process, you are ready to let it all dry.

An especially important part of this process of releasing is to remember to fill the void left by all you let go. A remarkably simple, and oh so powerful way to do this is for you to take a few moments between layers as you let them dry and turn your attention to your candle. Let your gaze fall on the flickering light. As the golden flame softens in your gaze, imagine it moving into that place inside of you that has just released the energy of each word. Take several moments, purposefully and with your sacred intent, inhale the golden light and allow it to ignite the beauty that you are bringing in to fill the void.

If you choose to later, you can spray it with an art fixative, frame it or tape it on the fridge, put it on your altar or hang it on a wall. This is a powerful piece of your art, of you. It tells your story and the story of these sacred words and all that you have released and replaced with them. Embrace it, all of it! It is you, manifest in beauty.

Your story, your art has power! Share it if you choose, especially if it is heavy and hard. Allow someone else to help carry some of it with you. When someone asks about your art piece, share your story. It may lead them to an eye-opening, a-ha moment that changes the direction of their own story.

Chapter Sixteen

FINDING THE LADDER

Be still and get to know the voice of Spirit
That speaks through the dark and the light.
Each one defining, neither surviving without the other.
Eat, drink, breathe, move, ponder, explore, examine.
Learn, believe, cling to nothing, take wonder in it all,
When you take the time to listen to Source, the One, the All.

*I*t's time to GET OFF THE SHELF!

Whatever your personal practice, it is all about connecting to that divine source of wisdom, joy and beauty that is within absolutely every one of us. It is always the right time when a new teacher comes along and never too late to learn more about the world, about life, about you.

My way in was the mystery school. There, I began to decipher the energies that played in the story of my life. I discovered the meaning of personal power and how we give it and take it consciously and unconsciously. I even found another trap to fall into – Cherla, that friend I mentioned earlier.

"Cut your hair, Vicki, it will look much better and more professional," she told me. "I've invited my hairdresser over to do my hair, why don't you come over and let her do yours?"

"Why not?" I thought to myself.

My hair was long, permed as in the Reba and Farrah days, pulled back in clips or under a visor, in a ponytail with a silver clip or funny bow. I had let a girl in the dorms my freshman year in college cut my hair – "Sassooned," I think they called it. More like "chopped off" – it was cut so short my head looked like a little pea balanced precariously on the top of my neck. I hated it and bought a "fall," an artificial attachment of long hair, but not quite a wig.

Now I was giving someone else the power to decide how my hair should look. Talk about self-conscious and full of doubt about my own worth in the eyes of someone else. After the haircut and color by Cherla's person, I looked up from the sink and saw my reflection in the window above. I cried into that sink as my hair was rinsed. I cried behind closed doors. I had loved my hair long and had never realized the "power and strength" it gave me. It was my individuality.

When my friend told me to wear black instead of brown, I did. She tried to help me see the chaos of my debt, but I didn't stop spending. I saw a bar so high I wasn't sure I would ever reach it but if she said I should jump, I said, "Sure, how high?" I set myself up on the shelf to try to be who I thought someone else thought I should be, as I saw in her, what I thought a successful woman was.

I couldn't believe how easy it was to give my power away even when no one, that I was aware of, was asking for it. What I also know now to be true, was that she was asking for it in her way, consciously or unconsciously as she tried to "help" me be a better me, in her opinion.

At home, life was in constant movement, with both children in college, a husband nearing retirement and my real estate career in full bloom. I was never still. When I graduated from the Mystery School, I wanted to give back to these amazing teachings that were beginning to find their way into my daily life. I didn't want my time with these teachers to end. I continued as a volunteer and mentor in the program. I kept myself busy and distracted from the real purpose of all I was learning... I set myself up on the shelf in service to these teachings, students, councils, events, expos. I kept myself going in the name of giving back and it was filling a big hole in my life, or what I thought was a hole.

After Ryan's passing in 2005, I stopped being active in my community. I finished my year as the outgoing chairman of the Board of Directors for the Clovis District Chamber of Commerce and that was the end of my volunteer work. Volunteering for and with Lynn Andrews Productions gave me an opportunity to stay connected to the Teachings I had come to know as my truth. Staying connected to the people in that circle fed our friendships, and fifteen to twenty years later I still call many of them friends. Being a mentor, holding space for the students in the school, kept me in touch with myself as I wobbled to maintain balance in my life. What was really missing was ME!

ME? I was fully present as the doing Vicki, sometimes being Vicki but missing the depth of Vicki, that place in me that held my heart's desire and fueled my soul's fire.

Even as I write today, my stomach tightens again and it becomes difficult to breathe, to continue. My whole being wants me to get up from this desk, close the computer and RUN! This story is clambering to be told and outside… the thunder rolls.

"Maybe I just need another Teacher… eh," I asked myself.

Would that just be another good distraction implemented in the name of "learning"? Or a way of practicing what I was preaching in the classes and workshops I was teaching while staying on the shelf in service to others?

Staying connected to my circle, while beginning the quest back to "me," I ventured out into the land of other teachings. I studied Peruvian shamanism and the beauty, power, and healing way of a mesa (altar). I had studied the use of altars in the mystery school and was now learning a new approach and practical ways in which to incorporate the mesa into a multitude of modalities from clearing negative energy to connecting with the ancestors and the stars, grounding in the energy of the elementals and the sacred mountains.

I learned to make drums. A big thank you to Cindy Green (aka Drumheart) for starting me on that journey. I studied drumming for shamanic journeying, divination and discovery with the Foundation for Shamanic Studies and learned a method of shamanic counseling that involved them all. I learned to listen to the voices in nature and how creativity is a source of inspiration and wisdom in the evolution of my own journey.

All the things I had encountered within the teachings of Lynn Andrews and the Sisterhood of the Shields, through the mystery school, had deepened the reservoir of my own experiences. So had learning from other amazing teachers: Michael Harner, Don Oscar Miro Quesada, Don Miguel Ruiz, and his family, HeatherAsh Amara, Dr. Steven Serr, Dr. Lewis Mehl Madrone, Beth Beurkens,

Josianne Antoinette. They were all saying the same things in different words, from different cultures. Some I resonated with deeply, others opened the doors of my comfort zone for me to try on different modalities to see which ones fit in my toolbox.

All taught about the sacred in all things, animate and inanimate. They taught about reverence and respect for the Earth and all her inhabitants. I moved between back-to-basics and advanced techniques. I began to develop my own point of view, my own truths as they lived in my life and through what I was beginning to teach. The more I learned, the farther down the ladder I came.

Each class, workshop and weekend led me closer to me, but it also filled time in my world that kept me from really looking for me, seeing me up there on that shelf albeit, a lower shelf now.

Each experience empowered the "me" I was becoming yet my eventual return to "real life" in the everyday work a day world would find me back up on the shelf doing the same things over, and over again, trying to find a balance between the spiritual blessings of the work I was learning and the world I had to live in.

Silence and alone time were precious commodities I had to leave home to find, but the call to home was always there, pulling me back to the places and people I loved. I was struggling with finding that balance. It was just so much easier to acquiesce me, to exit the scene in favor of shelf life, than it was to pull me forward into the life I felt calling from deep inside.

When we pull together all the pieces of ourselves into a new sacred being, we begin to discover who we are, not just what we have done in life. That is what I was learning to do; to bring the parts of me together into a new wholeness, into the space of where I wanted to be, into who I was becoming. I had found the key to my toolbox once again and I was getting reacquainted with all the different tools I had and was being exposed to. I was getting closer to the ladder.

I never imagined I could journey to the past and discover why my mother carried so much anger around with her. It was buried just far enough beneath the surface of her that it could be intensely felt but rarely seen. I learned how destructive that underlying anger could be as it came out in words meant to compliment but was actually a backward way of showing judgment and disappointment.

In one of the exercises I learned, we were asked to draw words out of an envelope and then paint the energy of that word. We were asked to create a sacred space to do this work and to make it a conscious act, not a reactional one. I would light my candle, call in the muses, and draw a word from the envelope. I drew the word mother.

"Oh, hell no. Not! I am not painting my mother," screamed that resistant voice in my head. In that moment of rising exasperation, I heard that still voice that surfaces when I am in a space where I can listen. *"The word is mother, not your mother!"*

Recall my earlier mention of when my mom said, "Gee you look nice in those white pants today, but maybe a darker pair would look even better." My translation: black would make my Rubenesque figure appear smaller.

With this exercise, the entire energy of that long-ago experience changed immediately. I painted a large, Rubenesque woman dressed all in red, sitting on the ground cradling a tiny baby on her drawn-up knees. It was so freeing, releasing that energy I had been carrying around in a bag of anger. I was myself, unconsciously stuffing that same anger around my feelings about my own mother. A beautiful ah-ha moment that had me out of that muck and blossoming as the lotus does when the sun's rays give life to the mud.

When we engage the mind in matters of Spirit, oftentimes fear or doubt will arise because the ego/mind cannot comprehend the realm of Spirit and it becomes fearful and confused. The ego, which is the mind (edging God out), lives in the realm of time. Time is a construct of the mind. It is the way we function and move through the experience of this dimension of consciousness that we call physical life or the third dimension of reality. The mind records the experiences of physical reality via the tool of time.

When "deep shit" happens, in my experience, my mind records it. When it slams me hard enough, that record just keeps playing over and over in my mind. If our minds can only record our physical reality in terms of time, then when we go over and over something in our mind, are we rewinding time?

No, I don't think so. I think we are "out of time," but not as in reached the end of or too late. We are simply no longer in the NOW. We have moved into the past and get stuck in a loop trying to guess what could be or should have been. When we begin to loop what will be because of a trauma or just a string of bad words, we have left the NOW and moved into the future.

Here is something I know for sure… It is important for us to stay in our feelings and, as my dear friend Kate would say, "Feel 'em, 'cuz there is no doubt that you will know exactly what you're all about down the road. We usually think we know, but man, pain is a great introducer to our real selves."

In the end, we only have ourselves to face in the mirror each day. Doubt, fear, anger, blame – all the negative emotions that play with us – are just rungs on the ladder, taking us higher up the shelf. They are the great distractors that keep us from living, keep us buried under the pile of rocks they create for us to carry around in this lifetime. They keep us on the shelf. Remember, it is in the movement that we find the change, as Christine Stevens reminds us again, "It is the process of participation that creates change."

When you get out of your own way and allow Spirit to move through you, as the divine you that you truly are, joy, laughter, wonderment, and gratitude become your companions. They are "friends" that will show you the ladder when you can't find it and encourage you to slide down with both feet. Stepping on each rung can offer you time and opportunity to change your mind and start to climb back up.

Change is constant, as our ancestors have continuously told us, and we will no doubt repeat to our heirs. "The world is changing." Our way off the shelf is to find that pure place where we reside in our own truth. It takes courage and strength to stay there. Use all the techniques and tools you can learn in this lifetime, on this earth schoolhouse, to get off your shelf.

A Way Off the Shelf: Drum Wisdom

"It's time to stop thinking of the drum as
just a musical instrument.

Start thinking of the drum as a recreational tool
for every family,

a wellness tool for every retiree, and an educational tool
for every classroom. "

–Remo Belli, the Founder of Remo Drums, Inc.

My toolbox was easier to get into now. A friend recommended that I get out my big drum and try writing out these feelings as I drummed. Kate told me years ago that I could sit with my drum, clear my mind... and drum. To let go of what was all around me and tap into what was going on inside of me.

"Drum, listen, feel, and then write. Write what the drum tells you. Write what you are feeling deep within the beat of the drum. Write the resonance of the moment when you connect with the Divine within you and hear the messages carried on the beat of your drum," she suggested.

Drums can be great companions and a source of unbiased wisdom. Try it sometime. If you don't have a drum, you can put a cardboard box in your lap and use your hands for drumming. Once you have settled into "your" rhythm, let the drum know what is on your mind, pose a question if you like. The key here is for you to LISTEN with your heart, not your head. Write whatever comes up, unfiltered and unedited. It may not make any sense to you at all, or it may just be that ah-ha you need in that moment.

201

Epilogue

BEGIN AGAIN
(BREAKING DOWN THE SHELF)

Crusader's shield laid down to rest,
The need to win released.
Live in silent witness, in quiet sanctuary.
From my heart, from deep within
I count each day's lesson learned.
Compassion, sorrow, anger, tears, blend into new dimensions.
Old feelings find no place, new life grows in opened space
Where dreams reshape funneled visions
And ladders rungs split, divisions escaping into reality
Softening yesterday's dismay with tomorrow's rainbows.
Speak loves new truth, let freedom reign,
Padlock-chained warrior's heart released.

I must talk myself through everything from that centered place within me that holds all the answers, to make heart-driven choices... where do I go from here?

1999 was one of my lightbulb years. 2005 brought financial freedom and unfathomable grief. Searching for and trying to expand my life and reconnect with my marriage all seemed so far away. I didn't know how to move forward. I was still on a treadmill running with the proverbial hamsters in a constant state of movement. I had not mastered how to live life. I was still reacting to it.

Peeling back the layers of what was then, I began to look at what I wanted life to be moving forward. I needed a purpose, a way to live more fully as me – not just as a mom, wife, daughter, sister, Realtor, advocate, or friend. I needed to learn how to live truthfully as me, to live intentionally each day, even in each moment, with each decision I made.

I wanted to live and move through life grace-fully. You may have heard about this thing called the Law of Deliberate Creation. It is the purposed focusing of thought with the intention of feeling alignment with one's own desire. I took this idea to heart and began to intentionally create the life I wanted to live.

Through the magnificent teachings I was blessed to find from so many wonderful men and women, I became aware of my own deepest desires, my dreams, and my values. I read and wrote and circled myself in a way I never knew existed. I made a commitment to try to live each day intentionally, to mindfully choose where I would exert time and energy and what thoughts would fill my mind. I picked up the reins of my own life. I moved into the driver's seat and discovered that I held the key to Getting Off the Shelf!

I began to dream big, designing my own destiny welcoming resistance as an opportunity, not an obstacle. I heard that often still voice whisper once again as it pulled on my heart, "There's more, you know. GET OFF THE SHELF!"

It takes courage to make changes and I love what Mary Ann Radmacher says: "Courage doesn't always roar. Sometimes courage is the quiet voice at the end of the day saying, 'I will try again tomorrow.' I had to put my 'try' back on and design my life in ways that fueled my joy and fed my creative spirit, hold fast to the boundaries I was rebuilding and I had to remember what peace there may be in silence.

Today I am still learning, I still find myself on that shelf, but I have more tools to break it down, a little more each time. The shadows that circle my life, our world, still play with my resolve and challenge me to remember to put me first, to enliven my days with new creativity and to love, always love those who bless me with their presence in my life.

May you find your path, joy on your journey and love and light along the way.

In the stillness before the sunrise,

when the world turns from dark to dawn,

a tiny bird sings joyfully in the distance…

"Good morning world, where are the worms?"

Namasté

Wisdom Evolution
Nurturing Body, Mind, Heart & Soul

ABOUT THE AUTHOR

*V*icki Dobbs is an Inspirator of Everyday Awareness, an Instigator of Spontaneous Stories, and a Connoisseur of Creativity. She walks a Path of Heart while co-creating with the Divine, while encouraging others to explore the magnificence of their own being-ness. She opens existential gateways for individuals to face their challenges and embrace them as the great teachers that they are. Her goal is to see everyone walk in beauty and balance every day of their lives empowered by the voice of their own authentic truth.

Through Wisdom Evolution and Sacred Wisdom Workshops, Vicki creates opportunities for you to explore deep, personal change through experiential classes, ceremony, sacred art, and story so that you may create your life intentionally. Her workshops are strongly rooted in the belief that when one connects with their own truth – that authentic voice inside that says YES – they touch the Divine within them that sparks their passion, ignites their joy and takes them to new levels of being.

As an Elder, Teacher, Award-winning Businesswoman and Spiritual Entrepreneur, Life Coach, Best-selling Author and Crafter of Sacred Art and Tools, Vicki perceives life's journey as an ever-upward spiraling ascension of the human spirit leading you to wisdom, wholeness, and authenticity.

Vicki was trained in the Harner Method of Shamanic Counseling and the Pachakuti Mesa Tradition of Cross-Cultural Shamanism. She is a Graduate Teacher and Mentor with the Lynn Andrews Center for Sacred Arts and Training, and an Artist of the Spirit Certified Spiritual, Energetic and Life Coach. Gratitude and grace, sprinkled with humility and humor, are the medicine she brings to the world.

Please visit Vicki's website for a special gift and join her Facebook community for updated information on her art, books, journals, online classes, projects, and workshops currently available to participate in or bring to your community.

Vicki L. Dobbs

Author, Teacher, Guide, Connoisseur of Creativity

Email: Vicki@vickidobbs.com

Visit: vickidobbs.com

facebook.com/SacredWisdomTeachings

https://www.instagram.com/vickidobbs/

Contact Vicki: 559-269-7653

ACKNOWLEDGMENTS

My heart overflows with Gratitude...

I am thankful to so many for their guidance, support, and encouragement as I continued this journey called writing.

I am grateful as always, for my family, who stand behind me, supporting and encouraging me to pursue new ideas, sometimes impossible appearing goals, and mystic dreams. I couldn't do this without them.

This book started with a sacred vision and has been nursed and fed by so many. I offer a shout out and so much gratitude to:

Christine Kloser who opened my eyes to the transformational journey.

To my dear friend and teacher, Lynn Andrews, for telling me that "I am a storyteller."

To Shanda Trofe for always reminding me that deep down inside, I have the answers.

To Dawn Montefusco, who helped me own my authentic voice and become a better writer with it.

To Devra Jacobs who has opened, and still opens today, gateways that stretch my comfort zone and allow my light to shine.

To Donna Kozik who told me I could, showed me I should, and pushed me off the ledge into doing it.

To all of you, thank you for all your encouragement, support, and energetic edits. I Love you guys. I am grateful for you all!

~Vicki Dobbs

Made in the USA
Las Vegas, NV
25 August 2022

54008374R00125